Comfort In Times of Grief

Wilfred (Wilf) R. Kent

xulon PRESS

Copyright © 2004 by Wilfred R. Kent
TWM International Publishers

Comfort In Times of Grief
by Wilfred R. Kent

Printed in the United States of America

ISBN 1-594678-79-0

All rights reserved under International Copyright Law. The author guarantees all contents are original and do not infringe upon the legal rights of any other person or work. Contents and/or cover may not be reproduced in whole or in part in any form without the express written permission of the Author. The views expressed in this book are not necessarily those of the publisher.

Unless otherwise indicated, all Scripture quotations are from the Authorized King James Version. Other quotations are from the New International Version (NIV), Copyright © 2003 by the Zondervan Corporation. The Living Bible (TLB), Copyright © 1971 by Tyndale House Publishers, and the New King James Version (NKJV), Copyright © 1997 by Thomas Nelson Bibles; Strong's Exhaustive Concordance Of The Bible, Copyright © 1890 by Abington-Cokesbury Press; New American Standard (NASB), Copyright © 2002 by Zondervan direct translations from the Greek.

TWM International Publishers
Today's World Ministries, Inc.
Turning Point Guidance & Counseling Services
International College Of Biblical Counseling

Visit our web sites at

- LifeStrategyinc.com
- WilfKent.org

www.xulonpress.com

ACKNOWLEDGEMENT

Special recognition is given to those who so tirelessly dedicated their talents in making this publication possible. This includes:

Jean Shockley	–	Proof-reading and editing
Angela Hass	–	Proof-reading and editing
Sally Barlow	–	Cover design
John Struve	–	LifeStrategyinc.com

and the many people whose life experiences have served as valuable examples.

DEDICATION

I dedicate this book in memory of my beloved wife Donna and to my children Michelle, Adrienne, Stephen and Jennifer, their spouses and the grandchildren they have borne to us. Your love, patience, encouragement and sacrifices made this book possible.

TABLE OF CONTENTS

THE LOVE STORY	(Chapter, Page)	*THE STRUGGLES OF FAITH*
Not Good For Man To Be Alone	**(01, 23)**	The Assault On Faith
Jungle Stud And Amazon Seductress	**(02, 29)**	The Doubt Of Faith
Discovering Each Other	**(03, 35)**	The Test Of Faith
The Great Escape	**(04, 41)**	The Shout Of Faith
Before The Happily Ever After	**(05, 47)**	The Anchor Of Faith
A Marriage Made In Heaven	**(06, 53)**	The Logic Of Faith
A Thankless Job	**(07, 59)**	The Abounding Faith
A Lateral Shift	**(08, 65)**	The Seduction Of Faith
Be Quiet And Go To Sleep	**(09, 71)**	The Ambivalence Of Faith
I Hate This Job	**(10, 77)**	The Words Of Faith

Comfort In Times of Grief

Walking In Divine Favor	**(11, 83)**	The Aids Of Faith
Stinking Hippies	**(12, 89)**	The Boldness Of Faith
EZ Street	**(13, 95)**	The Foolishness Of Faith
From EZ Street To Big Time	**(14, 101)**	The Wait Of Faith
Pain In The Grass	**(15, 107)**	The Peace Of Faith
A Love Letter To God	**(16, 113)**	The Risk Of Faith
Through The Wilderness Barefooted	**(17, 119)**	The Liberty Of Faith
Guess What Happened	**(18, 125)**	The Fluctuation Of Faith
Family Get-to-gathers	**(19, 131)**	The Disappointment Of Faith
One Adventure We Didn't Count On	**(20, 137)**	The Endurance Of Faith
A King And His Consort	**(21, 143)**	The Persistence Of Faith
A Peek Into Heaven	**(22, 149)**	The Cry Of Faith

Ears To Hear	**(23, 155)**	The Glories Of Faith
It Is Well With My Soul	**(24, 161)**	The Product Of Faith
The Refining Fires	**(25, 169)**	The Wilderness Of Faith
I Think It's Over, And Then ...	**(26, 175)**	The Revitalization Of Faith
A Legacy For Our Children	**(27, 181)**	Insights Through Faith

PREAMBLE

<u>Comfort In Times Of Grief</u> is an apt title for this book. It is a story of love and the struggles of faith. *The Love Story* element dates back to the beginning of the author's time and proceeds to the present. It traces the forty-four year history of God's leading in the lives of two people, their trials and the building of an outstanding relationship. Marriage can either be an entrance to an earthly Eden or the snare of infernal torment. This story outlines a happy marriage that was built through many sacrifices.

The Struggles Of Faith is an attempt to reconcile one's faith with the harshness of reality. The time frame is the present and encompasses a trying period of six months. It started as an essay of 300 words written by the hospital bed of my wife, who was struggling for her life on chemotherapy. During her four-month illness that ushered her into God's presence, twenty-six chapters were written forming the contents of this book. These struggles are recorded as WOW, an acronym for Words Of Wisdom. God often uses trail to bring about His purposes. A person that is unable to benefit from such trial forfeits that benefits that God has in store and is liable to repeat difficult trials of a similar nature. WOW, these are WordsOfWisdom we can live by.

Both the historical *Love Story* and the *Struggles of Faith* meet in the final chapters, integrating them into a unified whole, that brings hope to the grieving. Some have suggested titles like, <u>Grief Relief</u>, <u>Hope In Times Of Hopelessness</u>, <u>Beyond Despair</u> and <u>Insights On Faith</u>. Whatever the title, it is my sincere prayer that our love story and the struggles of faith and courage that have been our lot, will engender hope for those that may be walking through their valley of darkness.

Blessed be God, even the Father of our Lord Jesus

Christ, the Father of mercies, and the God of all comfort; Who comforts us in all our tribulation (troubles), *so that we may be able to comfort them which are in any trouble, by the comfort wherewith we ourselves are comforted of God.* (2 Corinthians 1:3-4)

Wilfred (Wilf) R. Kent

FOREWORD

Many preachers and counselors talk about the "Christian Walk" and things of God but in this "Love Story", Wilfred Kent the author and my friend, opens his heart to reveal a passion not only for what the Bible has to say about faith and trust in God, but also for what God might just do about it.

Dr. Kent, as always and even more so during the illness of his beloved Donna, is dedicated to the search for the God of the Bible who acts TODAY. Such a search is dangerous. Theology is safe as long as it is kept in the realm of discussion and incarcerated in the confines of academia.

As they traveled and ministered, Wilf and Donna were required to place their faith and trust in Him for supply. By His grace, they passed those tests with top honors. But then came Donna's medically declared terminal illness, a different test revealing a new realm of faith. The toughest test for any beloved.

This wonderful true story documents the details of that test. The vision at the heart of this book is different. It reveals a craving for more of God despite the wrenching pain of separation. To the Roll Call of Faith, added, are the names Wilfred and Donna Kent.

<u>Comfort In Times Of Grief</u> will be a source of encouragement for everyone that may have struggles with their Christian Walk.

With appreciation

Ivan Vorster, M.S.
Sheriffs Chaplin,
Santa Barbara County, CA

FOREWORD

When I first read the manuscript, I couldn't shake the felling that the ending was all wrong. What sort of story ends with the death of the heroine? What was God thinking? Surely, it would have been much more productive and to His greater glory to heal this His dedicated handmaiden. But as I continued over days and weeks to mediate on the subject, I came to realize Professor Kent's true theme and the one he wrote the book to promote. I erred greatly, because I knew not the scriptures nor the power of God. He is the God of the Living, not the dead!

Another "feel-good" story of a miraculous healing would be powerful, but not as powerful as the story of a God Who defeats death, raises the dead to life and sustains the living through death. Chances are, all of us will experience the loss of a loved one. Professor Kent's testimony details the loss of one's beloved and miraculous hope that springs from no earthly source. It is a hope born of faith securely fixed upon the immutability of God's Word. How much more life-giving then is this tale than the one I would have imagined?

Thank you Professor Kent for writing the story with the wrong ending. Thank you Lord for destroying the last enemy, Death.

Sincerely

Angela Hass, B.A.
USA Director
International College Of Biblical Counseling

INTRODUCTION

Since I was a lad of fourteen, I prayed that the Lord would bring someone into my life that would aid and abet the calling that God had on my life. Solomon declared that he *Who finds a wife finds a <u>good thing</u>, and obtains favour of the LORD.* (Proverbs 18:22) Armed with that promise I searched for ten years looking for my <u>good thing</u>. Since her commitment to Jesus at age five, she too felt called to missions. Her prayer was that the Lord would lead her to a man that would not work at cross-purposes to her calling. Resting in the assurance that *<u>no good thing</u> will he withhold from them that walk uprightly* (Psalms 84:11), she patiently waited. So it was that when I first saw her, it was love at first sight. I was convinced that this was my <u>good thing</u> that I had prayed for.

We were in our final year of college, she at nurse's training and I in seminary. Our courtship was by no means serene. Her parents had other plans for her life and I was seen as a villain that would disrupt their plans. That I did! Even though I was a perfect gentleman at all times, my presence was as welcome as nuclear waste. They were convinced that I was that <u>no good thing</u> which she unfortunately "dragged home". It was sad that as adults we had to elope to get married. We began our life together with school debts, parental opposition and many responsibilities. Despite the opposition, we knew that God was directing us. These were the fires that forged our love into a strong marriage that would carry us through many trials.

We became best friends as well as lovers and had the highest respect for one another. As colleagues, we labored together, teaching God's Word on a variety of subjects that pertained to marriage, well being and interpersonal relationships. What we taught from the platform, we lived in our lives. It was more than academic professionalism or theological rhetoric to us. We proved that the principles God established worked.

The miles we logged in four decades cannot be numbered. We enjoyed the fellowship of long-term friends that lived in many parts of the world. Often we talked about making our headquarters here, or there or somewhere, perhaps anywhere. Ours was a fairy-tale relationship that was to carry us into the fall season of our lives. Over the many miles and years, He who brought us together never left us. Even in our darkest hours, He was there all the time. What a mighty God we serve!

This then, is a love story that could very well be your testimony. It is a real life drama that illustrates the struggles of faith that overcomes every obstacle, including death.

It is my earnest prayer that wealth of experience and wisdom that the years bring, will be a source of encouragement to all that are facing trials.

... Be strong and of a good courage; be not afraid, neither be thou dismayed: for the LORD thy God is with thee whithersoever thou goest. (Joshua 1:9)

Wilfred (Wilf) R. Kent

PROLOGUE - DONNA'S UNEDITIED DIARY

It was Donna's intent to chronicle the event of her illness, her attitude and emotions, and her uncomplicated trust in God and hope for recovery. Just one week into her chemotherapy, her fatigue became so great that she was no longer able continue. These are her last written words.

"It is Friday – appointment with Dr. McMahon (the oncologist).
"Dad is in Winnipeg (on tour) – All the children are going to the appointment with me.
"I am removed from the children and Dr. tells me I have acute Leukemia.
"Prognosis is 30-60 days without treatment.
"We go to the conference room to tell the children.
"Much pain and tears although we thought we were prepared for it.
"Prayed together.
"Called Dad home. How hard for him. He is alone to process this.
"Immediate decision to start treatment tomorrow.
"God clearly directs me to Porter Hospital. Confirmation by another.
"My peace is overwhelming, as if this is being spoken over someone else.
"Not denial – deep peace. Thankful I will be with family.
"Admission to hospital is hairy. Nobody knows where I am to go.
"Tired physically and emotionally. Dearest Wilf, so strong but hurting so.
"Psalms 112:7-8 We all stand on it. So many scriptures bring

peace and faith!

"I.V. started. Blood taken. Lots of information. Didn't sleep to well.

"It would seem this is the day we are all processing.

"All of us crying from deep within, yet declaring with our lips our confidence in the Lord.

"How can you have so much peace and yet so much pain?

"The team of Drs. coming in many ways speaking death and complications, on the other hand scripture and encouragement negates every evil word spoken.

"The pick is put into my shoulder ... I was very apprehensive.

"The nurse... knows Jesus.

"Before starting (we) hold our hands and prays a powerful presence.

"Then she gets into the vein slick and easy and we continue to have good results.

"My first bag of chemo begins.

"I feel nothing but an overwhelming sense of peace.

"This is all about life not death.

"Everything is a bit intimidating but I know that over a month it will be ………..

Surely he shall not be moved for ever: the righteous shall be in everlasting remembrance. He shall not be afraid of evil tidings: his heart is fixed, trusting in the LORD.
(Psalms 112:7-8)

Chapter 1

NOT GOOD FOR MAN TO BE ALONE & THE ASSAULT ON FAITH

THE LOVE STORY - Not Good For Man To Be Alone

Five years of college and seminary is a long and expensive haul. It can best be described as an uphill wagon pull over a rough road. This is particularly true for someone that has to make his own way without outside support. And so it was that every summer I would find any type of employment available to me and save every cent for tuition and school related expenses. It was in my third year that I found work in the far north of British Columbia, Canada. The pay was very good because of the isolation and danger involved. Six men and a cook were transported by helicopter into isolation that seemed far off the edge of the earth. I was one of the "lucky" ones that was abandoned there for four months. Our job was to repair and maintain high voltage power lines that crossed the Rocky Mountains. The Lord spared my life on two particular occasions, and I knew that His plan for me could not be thwarted.

Amid the beauty of virgin timber and snow-capped mountains, the solitude was often overwhelming. Living with six smelly men that spent their off time drinking and gambling away their paychecks, was even more isolating. I had nothing of interest in common with the crew and my testimony was frequently berated. But it was good money and it would pay for my tuition. I spent many hours in solitary thought and communion with my Lord. I was in awe by the magnificence of His creation. It was here that I learned many valuable lessons. Among them, was that the smell of powder and perfume was much to be preferred to the stench of body odor and beer breath. Was it not God Himself that said, *It is not good for the man to be alone. I will make a helper suitable for him?* (Genesis 2:18) Then why am I here in this herd of smelly rogues?

I had been asking for God's direction for the coming year when the supply helicopter brought me a special delivery letter. It came from the registrar of a seminary with whom I had no contact. It was a mystery to me how they had found me in this forsaken wilderness, but it was a good indication that God had led them. I registered for transfer of credits and when my stint was complete, left the beautiful mountains and traveled three thousand miles to a place I had never been before.

It was our first weekend at seminary and a classmate and I went to church. Neither of us knew where we were going and arrived half way through the service. As we sat down the pastor announced, "Before I deliver what God has laid on my heart, Donna, who is a senior student at nurses college is going to minister to us in song." Instantly, I was captivated by her demeanor! She looked like a goddess to me, and it appeared that the dress she was wearing was grateful for having the opportunity of adorning her body. Before she completed the first verse and chorus of the song she was singing, I nudged my classmate and whispered, "I'm going to marry that girl!"

I didn't realize how prophetic that statement was to become. That evening I worked up the courage to ask if I could take her to the College and Career Class that met every Sunday evening. It was here that our date of forty-five years began. And yes, I now had incontrovertible proof that the fragrance of powder and perfume is much to be preferred to that of halitosis and body odor, a scent to which I had become accustomed.

Now WOW - The Assault On Faith

The report stunned us into silence. My companion of forty-four years was diagnosed with Acute Leukemia and given 30 to sixty days to live unless she had immediate chemotherapy. I had just arrived in Canada for a three-week series of meetings, when my wife Donna told me the shocking news. Forty-five years ago I went on a date that was seemingly endless, and now it appears that it may come to an end. I took the next flight home and that evening we were admitted into a Denver hospital. This was the start of our trek through a dark valley of uncertainty. I quickly sent an email message to my mailing list with an urgent message. It read, "Donna has been diagnosed with Acute Leukemia. She has been in chemotherapy for 48 hours. Please, we treasure your prayers".

Thoughts! Countless memories! Confusion! Fear! Overwhelming sorrow and pain! The news left our four married children and us completely dumfounded. A kick in the stomach would be a welcomed alternative. Where do we turn? Lord, I need your counsel!

We cannot deny the Lord His sovereignty. He is God. The Psalmist David was clearly committed to the will of God when he penned, *My frame was not hidden from you when I was made in the secret place. When I was woven together in the depths of the earth, your eyes saw my unformed body. All the days ordained for me were written in your book before one of them came to be. How precious to me are your thoughts, O God! How vast is the sum of them!* (Psalms 139:15-17) Who can withstand Him? Can the thing made demand of its Maker, *why hast thou made me thus?* We are twice His, by reason of creation and purchased by redemption. We cannot deny our Lord's sovereignty and we will praise Him in sickness and in health. However, our Sovereign God has given us many promises. It is His good pleasure to respond to those that take Him at His word. He has ordained mortal man to move His sovereign hand! It is His pleasure to respond to those that call upon Him. ... *prove me now herewith, saith the LORD of hosts, if I will not open you the windows of heaven, and pour you out a blessing, that there shall not be room enough to receive it.* (Malachi 3:10) *And call upon me in the day of trouble: I will deliver thee, and thou shalt glorify me.* (Psalms 50:15) *...the righteous... He shall not be afraid of evil tidings: his heart is fixed, trusting in the LORD. His heart is established, he shall not be afraid, until he see his desire upon his enemies.* (Psalms 112:6-8) *And Jesus went...teaching...preaching... and healing all manner of sickness and all manner of disease among the people.* (Mathew 4:23) *Beloved, I desire that in all things thou shouldest prosper and be in health, even as thy soul prospers.* (3 John 1:2)

In this we are resolute! Never allow your theological hang-ups to so bind you that you cannot do your thing! Never limit the power of God, as did our predecessors. *Yea, they turned back and tempted God, and limited the Holy One of Israel.* (Psalms 78:41) *So we see that they could not enter in because of unbelief.* (Hebrews 3:19) Have faith in this; He has created us for life and not for death! *...we are his workmanship, created in Christ Jesus unto good works, which God hath before ordained that we should walk in them.* (Ephesians 2:10) His sovereign will includes our health and well-being as well as our eternal salvation.

We are praying for Donna's quick and complete healing.

He that created the red and white blood cells, the platelets and all that make up the blood, is well able to fix them! Never doubt His ability to hear your prayers and to work miracles. The cancer manual speaks of death. The Bible speaks of life! Whose report will you believe? We shall believe the report of the Lord! Thank you for walking in faith with us!

Then shall thy light break forth as the morning, and thine health shall spring forth speedily: and thy righteousness shall go before thee; the glory of the LORD shall be thy rereward. Then shalt thou call, and the LORD shall answer; thou shalt cry, and he shall say, Here I am. (Isaiah 58:8-9)

WOW! These are WordsOfWisdom we can live by!
><)))*>

A Personal Challenge And Prayer Of Commitment

Has your faith been shaken because of bad news? Are you afraid of the future? Trust Him. His mind is full of you! This is the import of Psalms 8:4 *What is man, that thou art mindful of him? and the son of man, that thou visitest him?*

"Dear Lord: I know that nothing escapes Your attention. In our darkest times we have witnessed Your hand at work on our behalf. Surely, we occupy a special place in Your heart and mind. As we have trusted You in the past, we now place our faith and future in Your hands. Thank You that You hear me Lord. This I ask in the name of Jesus, our Redeemer. – Amen"

Chapter 2

JUNGLE STUD AND THE AMAZON SEDUCTRESS & THE DOUBT OF FAITH

THE LOVE STORY – The Jungle Stud And The Amazon Seductress

I had two significant goals for my life. The first was to complete my studies and the second was to get married. It may have been the other way around, but both seemed equally urgent to me. I carried a full time job while at seminary. Classes ran from 8 a.m. through noon, and the job at the Corrugated Box Factory from 2 until 10. Homework and study came after that. Her schedule was equally as demanding. Her classes ran during the day and floor duty came forever after that. Her mother made sure to dominate what free time she did have. We had precious few moments to work on our romance. The College and Career Youth Group following the Sunday evening service offered the best time to explore each other's past. Here we discovered some remarkable similarities that only engendered my resolve that she was the girl!

As a young lad of fourteen I made my commitment to Jesus at a small country church that sat high on a hill. It was near here that I was baptized in a muddy barnyard pond among the ducks, geese and cow paddies. And it was also here that I received my missionary call to the continent of Africa. Sitting one afternoon on the front step, I looked down on the green hills that stretched off into the horizon, and could envision Africa. Although I had never seen pictures of that continent, the appeal was so strong that I would have abandoned everything on the spot to go. However, my fervor was dampened by reality and I knew that a long bumpy road lay ahead of me if I was ever to get there. This became the driving force behind my years of study.

She too, vividly recalls the day that as a child she walked down the isle of a city church to ask Jesus into her life. It was an experience that remained etched in her memory throughout life. At the age of 10 she was teaching children Bible stories on a flannel-graph board. She became so good at it, that during the summer months she would go from church to church teaching the stories during Vacation Bible School. It was here that she began to hone her teaching skills.

She too, was called to Africa. There was no question in her mind that some day she would be there. Her preparation began with vocal and piano lessons at an early are. She became so accomplished at the piano that Youth For Christ used her as their pianist for the rallies, and she traveled with one of Canada's leading evangelists. One day a nationally known bandleader came to the city and held auditions for artists. Donna went to the try-outs and was offered a position in his orchestra. "What an opportunity to achieve wealth and stardom," she thought. But that would mean traveling about the world in a secular environment. More importantly, that would mean an end to her calling. That is what I admired so much about her. She willing exchanged self-seeking stardom and wealth for the call of God.

We were only a year from graduation and I could hardly keep my mind on my studies. I was completely "zonked out of my gourd" by my fortune. I would sit over my books but my imagination was seduced by dreams of the future. I envisioned her as the "Amazon Seductress" and I myself as the "Jungle Stud" that together would carve out a "Brave New World" in some remote part of the earth. What romance! What adventure! What potential! WOW! Then I would snap back to reality with a stinging thought, "Your fantasies are a waste of time! You still have your Greek vocabulary to memorize. Get at it!"

Now WOW - The Doubt Of Faith

Plastic bags filled with lethal poison hang high above her hospital bed, dripping death into her veins. Death to the killers of healthy blood cells, and death to death itself! During the long hours I muse about the subject of faith.

Theologically, *faith is the substance of things hoped for, the evidence of things not seen.* (Hebrews 11:1) Technically, faith is the simple process of believing God and acting on His Word. I had taught that on more occasions than I can remember. It was more than a theological concept to us. We lived it. For more than twenty years we ministered in South Africa, Malawi, Zimbabwe, Poland, Singapore, Malaysia, The UK, and throughout Canada and the USA. During that time we carried no health insurance, had no church support groups or fund raising programs. We firmly believed that if it was God's project He would fund it! Indeed He did. We were never hungry, sick or abandoned. Our motto is summed up in the refrain of an old hymn, *Faith, mighty faith the promise sees, and looks to God alone; Laughs at impossibilities and cries, IT SHALL BE DONE!*

But now, in the long hours of quietness I ponder whether that was faith or mere presumption, a kind of pseudo-spiritual denial of reality. What is faith all about anyway? Is it some pious recitation or some magic formula that we chant to make it happen? Whatever it may be that we wish to happen? I'm prepared for death, but not right now. "Not right now Lord!" Doubts flood my mind, thoughts of confusion, fear. "She looks well" the enemy whispers, "but it belies the serious nature of her illness. Listen to what the professionals tell you and stop living in denial!" And as I listen to his rationale, the torment becomes overwhelming.

Driving home late one evening, the enemy accosted me mercilessly in an audible voice. "What are you going to do now, Wilf? What are you going to do now? Your wife is going to die; the hospital costs are going to bankrupt you; you have had to cancel all your meetings and now you are unemployed, and furthermore, at your age, who in their right mind is going to ask for your services?" he said. I heard the enemy clearly! The words came from my own mouth and I instantaneously knew where they were coming from. My doubts had made me an accomplice of the devil.

Faith is a sword easily wheeled when things are going well. We testify to mighty faith when all our needs are well supplied and sing of heaven when we are strong. Life is a rosy cakewalk in the park with Jesus, when everywhere we turn, we see His blessings. Peace, joy, adventure, happiness, supply and more are part of His blessing to us. This is the rightful heritage of the child of God, but it is not faith.

It is when our steps lead us down some troublesome path, that faith must be exercised. Do we now doubt His tender mercies, who through life has been our guide? No! A thousand times no! Anger wells up within me, not at God who allowed the trial but at my own doubts that impugn His character. Resentment builds against the fear and lies that the enemy inflicts upon me. And I remind him that the wrath of God is revealed against all *who exchanged the truth of God for the lie...* (Romans 1:25) *"God is not a man, that He should lie, Nor a son of man, that He should repent. Has He said, and will He not do? Or has He spoken, and will He not make it good? Behold, I have received a command to bless;*

He has blessed, and I cannot reverse it." (Numbers 23:19-20) After all, are we not on the Lord's side? Is there any circumstance greater than He! So I embolden myself with His word and His numberless promises of presence, protection, provision and posterity. Once that mental and emotional battle is won, we can sit back in calm repose and commit the outcome to Him!

When all around our soul gives way, it's Christ who is our strength and stay! "Lord, You are God! How blessed we are to know and serve You! If we had a thousand lives, we would invest each one in You. Our heart is enlarged with worship and our lips are filled with praise toward You. How precious are our thoughts toward You. Blessed be Your name!"

Thus God, determining to show more abundantly to the heirs of promise the immutability of His counsel, confirmed it by an oath, that by two immutable things (His character and His word), *in which it is impossible for God to lie, we might have strong consolation, who have fled for refuge to lay hold of the hope set before us. This hope we have as an anchor of the soul, both sure and steadfast ...* (Heb. 6:17-19)

WOW! These are WordsOfWisdom we can live by! ><)))*>

A Personal Challenge And Prayer Of Commitment

If you are confused by what you see as reversals in your life, you need to refocus your vision on Jesus and not the circumstances of your life. *Looking unto Jesus the author and finisher of our faith ...lest ye be wearied and faint in your minds.* (Hebrews 12:2-3) *Don't yield your members as an instrument of unrighteousness unto sin: but yield yourselves unto God.* (Romans 6:13)

"Dear Lord: Your Word tells me that You have a plan for my life. Help me to endure the present so that I will not derail Your purposes for me. Help me to ... *trust in the Lord with all my heart.* (Proverbs 3:5-6) I will not lean unto my own understanding. I will acknowledge You in all my ways, You will direct my paths! I make this quality choice in the name of Jesus, - Amen!"

Chapter 3

DISCOVERING EACH OTHER & THE TEST ON FAITH

THE LOVE STORY – Discovering Each Other

Our courtship resembled the gestation period and labor pains of childbirth. Our times together were eked out between classes, work and parental responsibilities. How sparse and precious were our moments alone. I would drive an hour to see her for thirty minutes after her ward duty, then make the lonely drive back to my dormitory to prepare for the next day's classes.

Although we were captivated by our spiritual similarities, the personal differences were evident. She was reared in a modern city. I grew up on a remote farm that had no electricity, telephone or modern conveniences. As a lad, my version of running water was the five-gallon bucket I used to run to the well with. She was well educated in a large school. I attended a one room schoolhouse that accommodated the entire student body, all eight of us. I failed grade five, yet I was at the top of my class. This is because I was the only grade five student for miles around. She came from well-bred British stock. My stock were cows, pigs, chickens and all the farm animals that disadvantaged European immigrants tended. I saw the monochrome world in black and white. Her colors were indigo, chartreuse, vermilion, lavender and aquamarine. My color schemes were dark and uninviting, and from my vantage point, I saw her color tastes as plain noisy. Furthermore, she liked tea while my preferred choice of beverage was coffee.

I had no knowledge of meteorology but I was sharp enough to know that when a cold front collides with a warm front, tornadoes can spawn. Fog, drizzle, rain, hail, lightening and thunderstorms can also be produced. There were omens of rough weather ahead, but our sails were trimmed for the voyage.

It was clear why her parents objected to our relationship. The differences were too glaring. "It will never work," said her mother. But it did! "This is not of God! Your relationship is not His will," she reiterated. But it was. "You will stop seeing him," she demanded. I was a perfect gentleman and sought to honor her parents. So we did. But just for a while. By now, I was a college graduate of 24 and she a graduate nurse of 22, so we didn't. We saw something in each other that was not evident to her parents or the public.

Beneath the exteriors we saw characteristics that were most admirable. She saw my strength and loyalty. I saw her grace and tenderness. She saw my motivation and tenacious drive to achieve something. I saw her artistic and creative ability to make something beautiful. She admired my boldness and forthrightness, and I her gentle ability to accommodate and satiate. She had the unique ability to "pull my foot out of my mouth" with such dexterity, that to others it appeared as though that was the proper place for it. This is why I loved her so much.

We turned these obstacles into opportunities for growth. We both loved the Lord and were submissive to Him. Furthermore, we both had a "teachable spirit". Together our personalities would blend into "one flesh". As we assimilated many of each other's characteristics, we doubled in experience and character, and became one "new man".

Now WOW! - The Test Of Faith

I am well familiar with the testing procedure. As professor I have prepared many quizzes, tests and exams in the past four decades. During that time I had written and taught a curriculum of thirty-three college level courses and each required a standard of achievement. Students usually greet tests with the enthusiasm reserved for a root-canal at exam time. Fear of failure was the primary reason for their aversion. Tests however, are not designed to reward or punish students, but to insure that they understand the material taught. There are times that a student must repeat the same course of study. Only after the test is satisfactorily passed is the course complete. This may be academic prattle to most people, but as I sit by my wife's hospital bed, it is serious stuff to me. Now, the testing time is mine. How will my faith stand in the face of adversity? Frankly, I agree with my students. I don't like tests!

What is this thing called faith, and does it require a test to be proven? If faith is merely a subjective feeling, then I will have as many ups-and-downs in my Christian walk as does a pump handle. Alternatively, if faith is based on objective reality, then it will stand the test of time regardless of the circumstances. Rather than aversion, the Psalmist David welcomed his test with these words; *Examine me, O LORD, and prove me; Try my mind and my heart.* (Psalms 26:2) *Search me, O God, and know my heart: try me, and know my thoughts: And see if there be any wicked way in me, and lead me in the way everlasting.* (Psalms 139:23-24)

Belshazzar the King, was *weighed in the balances, and art found wanting.* (Daniel 5:22-27) God tried Israel at Marah...*and there He tested them, and said, "If you diligently heed the voice of the LORD your God and do what is right in His sight, give ear to His commandments and keep all His statutes, I will put none of the diseases on you which I have brought on the Egyptians. For I am the LORD who heals you.* (Exodus 15:25-26) Jesus told Peter that Satan had...*asked for you, that he may sift you as wheat.* (Luke 22:31) Peter spoke of the reality of trails when he challenged ...*Beloved, do not think it strange concerning the fiery trial which is to try you, as though some strange thing happened to you.* (1 Peter 4:12) James was more emphatic when he wrote, *My brethren, count it all joy when ye fall into <u>divers temptations</u>* [different kinds of testing]; *Knowing this, that the <u>trying</u>* [dokimeeon – testing, trial to establish trustworthiness] *of your faith worketh patience. But let patience have her perfect work, that ye may be perfect and entire, wanting nothing.* (James 1:2-4)

Joy? Count it all joy? In light of the serious nature of my circumstances, how can I "count it all joy?" The joy comes not from the circumstance but from the One who transcends the circumstance. This is clearly underscored in 1 Peter 1:6-9. *Wherein ye greatly rejoice, though now for a season, if need be, ye are in heaviness through <u>manifold temptations</u>* [all kinds of adversities]: *That the <u>trial</u> of your <u>faith, being much more precious than of gold</u> that perisheth, though it be tried with fire, might be found unto <u>praise</u> and <u>honour</u> and <u>glory</u> at the appearing of Jesus Christ.*

Faith is precious to God. The Greek word for precious is *teemay*, which means valuable, esteemed, dignified, honorable. God's purpose for the testing is to produce a faith that is praise worthy, honorable and full of glory. And so, submissively I pray, "Thank you Lord for refining my faith!" *Now no <u>chastening</u>* [paideia – education, training] *for the present seemeth to be joyous, but grievous: nevertheless afterward it yieldeth the peaceable fruit of righteousness unto them which are exercised thereby.* (Hebrews 12:11) *Blessed is the man that endureth <u>temptation</u>* [pirasmos - putting to the proof]: *for* when he is <u>tried</u> [dokeemos – acceptable, approved], *he shall receive the crown of life, which the Lord hath promised to them that love him.* (James 1:12)

WOW These are WordsOfWisdom we can live by!
><)))*>

A Personal Challenge And Prayer Of Commitment

Don't give into discouragement in the face of opposition. Never succumb to your fears. "Never, Never, Never give up!" (Winston Churchill) *Finally, my brethren, be strong in the Lord, and in the power of his might. Put on the whole armour of God, that ye may be able to stand against the wiles of the devil.* (Ephesians 6:10-11)

"Dear Lord: Forgive me for those times that I have become faint and weary in well doing. Help me to remember Your unfailing love and abiding presence. Help me to see the final product as I endure my current circumstances. I look to You as I ask this in the name of You Son Jesus, my Savoir – Amen!"

Chapter 4

THE GREAT ESCAPE & THE SHOUT OF FAITH

THE LOVE STORY – The Great Escape

More than enamored, I was inflamed with her love. My inamorata graduated two months before me and continued her twelve-hour shift of floor duty at the hospital. I couldn't understand why it was that every time we were together she fell into a deep sleep. I had pictured myself as an affable and sort of charming chap, but to her I must have been as exciting as a poached egg. She always appeared exhausted so I logically assumed that her work was getting to her. Not so.

Unbeknown to me was the pressure that she had to endure when she came home. Her mother, who had rested all day for the evening's drama, was waiting for her each time she came home. Till all hours of the morning she would point out the error of daughter's waywardness, at times with crying, shouting and bouts of self-pity. Later I would learn that she had endured this treatment for most of her life, adored in public but berated in private. The disapproval would continue until Donna would give in and appease her mother's demands. One morning Donna could not get out of bed. Her back and neck muscles became so rigid that she could not move. Her doctor was summonsed to the house who gave her a strong sedative and said, "Young lady, you are under a great deal of stress from some source. You must resolve your issues to keep this from reoccurring."

Seeking to bring some comfort, I found a stuffed-animal in a boutique window. It represented almost a week's wages, but putting my priorities aside I had it wrapped. Inside I placed a note that read: "This French poodle is named Froo. His name comes from Philippians 4:6-7. *Don't worry about anything, but in every thing by prayer and supplication with thanksgiving let your requests be made known unto God. And the peace of God, which passes all understanding, shall* keep (*froo-reh'-o*, it means to guard or fortify) *your hearts* (that is what you feel with) *and minds* (that is what you think with) *through Christ Jesus.* Be well soon my Darling – Wilf" Because I was not allowed near the house, I had it delivered by taxi. When mother received it at the door she was delighted, thinking it was for her.

One morning I arrived at the seminary to find a note in my mailbox. The curt message read, "I must leave now. Pick me up. Quickly!" Rather than going to class I walked into the Registrar's office and said, "Please don't ask me any questions. I am leaving school for a week. I will come back and complete my assignments. I will graduate and I'll willing bear any penalty." He didn't say a word. He just looked at me and knowingly smiled. He was well aware of the many young men mother ran off and the adage that had become common knowledge, "You get Donna; You get Momma!"

The Seminary Librarian loaned me her car, cash was borrowed from another source, a few of Donna's belonging were hurriedly tossed into the back seat and we drove off. We left her home, left the city, left the province, crossed the border and left the country. This was our great escape! Donna slept most of the thousand-mile journey. The steady hum of the tires and her peaceful breathing gave me ample time to reflect. "She sleeps because she finds in me a safe place! I will be that to her." My mind tried to make sense of the hurried events of that day. "How can what I am doing be right? This is silly. We are adults! What are we running from? What am I going to find when I get there? Where am I going? How am I going to face the music when I get back? Surely, there will be a song and dance that I will be required to orchestrate."

"Oh well, with God's help, I can do that. And for my precious cargo that rests so peacefully, I'll do anything," I mused!

Now WOW! - The Shout Of Faith

I sit silently by her bedside caressing her arm. Twelve long hours pass with less than ten short sentences spoken between us. Nausea, stomach cramps, body sores and a high fever are common side affects of such treatment, and I begin to wonder if the cure is not worse than the disease itself. "Lord, You tell me to rejoice in all things and shout for joy. But in view of the circumstances, how do I do that?"

A shout is a response to some form of stimuli. Shouts of victory volley throughout a stadium when the home team wins. Children shout with delight at an unexpected surprise. A warning of imminent danger is signaled by a shout. In the case of faith, however, there is nothing to shout about! As a matter of fact, all the scientific evidence points to dismal consequences. Despite the overwhelming odds and improbability of success, singing, shouting and dancing seems to be God's principal weapons against the enemy. There are examples in scripture that illustrate this.

The Children of Israel came against Jericho, a city fortified by impenetrable walls. God instructed Joshua to take the city with a trumpet-blast and the shouts of victory. *...So the people shouted when the priests blew the trumpets. And it happened when the people heard the sound of the trumpet,* *and the people shouted with a great shout, that the wall fell down flat ... and they took the city.* (Joshua 6:5-20)

For years the Midianites and the Amalekites; bitter enemies of Israel, plundered their villages and ravaged their crops. God chose an unlikely farm-laborer by the name of Gideon to defeat the marauding hordes. He also chose an unconventional method. Each soldier was armed with a torch, a clay vessel and a trumpet. They surrounded the camp during the night and at the trumpet sound, broke the vessels exposing the flaming torches. ... *they blew the trumpets, and brake the pitchers, and held the lamps in their left hands, and the trumpets in their right hands to blow withal: and they cried* (shouted out in an accosting manner), *The sword of the LORD, and of Gideon.* (Judges 7:19-20) It was dark and the enemy soldiers slew each other thinking them to be Gideon's army.

The Ammonites and Moabites arrayed themselves against Jehoshaphat, a righteous king of Israel. The overwhelming odds made victory impossible. His testimony makes this clear, *O our God, will You not judge them? For we have no power against this great multitude that is coming against us; nor do we know what to do, <u>but our eyes are upon You</u>.* (2 Chronicles 20:12) The Prophet Jahaziel encouraged them with these words. *Be not afraid nor dismayed by reason of this great multitude; for the battle is not yours, but God's ...Ye shall not need to fight in this battle: set yourselves, stand ye still, and see the salvation of the LORD with you* (2 Chronicles 20:17) Jehoshaphat believed God and in the face of impossible odds *...appointed singers unto the LORD, and that should praise the beauty of holiness... And when they began to sing and to praise, the LORD set ambushments against the children of Ammon, Moab, and mount Seir, which were come against Judah; and they were smitten.* (2 Chronicles 20:21-22)

Judah was surrounded by an ambush. Jeroboam's armies

were before them and behind them. Without God's intervention defeat was certain. ... *and the priests sounded with the trumpets. Then the men of Judah gave a shout: and as the men of Judah shouted, it came to pass, that God smote Jeroboam and all Israel before Abijah and Judah.* (2 Chronicles 13:14-15)

The evidence speaks of impossible odds, but our eyes are upon Him. God is not limited by forensic science. God is limited by unbelief. So in advance of victory, we give our shout of faith!

Sing...shout...be glad and rejoice with all the heart... the LORD, is in the midst of thee: thou shalt not see evil any more...Fear thou not...Let not thine hands be slack. The LORD thy God in the midst of thee is mighty; he will save, he will rejoice over thee with joy; he will rest in his love, he will joy over thee with singing. (Zephaniah 3:14-17) *But let all those rejoice who put their trust in You; Let them ever shout for joy, because You defend them; Let those also who love Your name Be joyful in You. For You, O LORD, will bless the righteous; With favor You will surround him as with a shield.* (Psalms 5:11-12)

WOW These are WordsOfWisdom we can live by! ><)))*>

A Personal Challenge And Prayer Of Commitment

The lyrics of a song popularized by Kenny Rogers, reflects a great deal of wisdom. "You gotta know when to hold them, know when to fold them, know when to throw them, when to walk away." Confused? Are you wondering what to do? Are you bewildered by your choices? A better plan of action is to hear the lyrics written by Jeremiah. *This is what the LORD says: "Stand at the crossroads and look; ask for the ancient paths, ask where the good way is, and walk in it, and you will find rest for your souls.* (Jeremiah 6:16)

"Dear Lord: I shall return to Your Word that outlines the ancient paths. Direct my steps and help me to make the right choices. I shall trust in You, whatever the outcome. Thank You that You hear me Lord. This I ask in Your name, Jesus – Amen."

Chapter 5

BEFORE THE HAPPILY EVER AFTER & THE ANCHOR OF FAITH

THE LOVE STORY – Before The Happily Ever After

Rumors regarding our disappearance ran rampant. "I can't believe that Wilf! Five years of study only to bail out three weeks before graduation? Can you believe that Donna would do such a thing? There is only one reason why they had to run. Just count the months!" The Pastor's wife entered the fray as the shocking news reverberated throughout the church community. "Disgraceful!" "Yes, disgusting! We need to tell others so that they can pray more effectively!"

The brouhaha fell silent and the embarrassment turned one-eighty degrees when I returned one week later, proving all gossip as unwarranted speculation. "Wilf, welcome back," smiled the Registrar, "I knew you would do it!" He had staked his professional reputation on my decision. "What an honor," I thought. "If for his sake alone, I must not fail." I completed all my assignments, attended the commencement exercises and received my degree. For the next three months I continued to work at the box factory. The long distance phone bills left me little choice. In the mean time, I tried to comfort Donna's Dad who now had to deal with his wife without a go-between. My attempts to bring resolution appeared to be working, but it only belied her true feelings.

We were married four months after our elopement. The small New England church was beautifully decorated and the ceremony simple. Both of our parents were there. I was shocked to see my parents arrive unexpectedly. They had driven three thousand miles to get there. Donna's mother hand stitched a magnificent wedding gown without measurements. It fit her perfectly. All indications pointed to a stellar day. Donna was stunning. She looked so happy. "Thank you Lord for granting my prayer and leading me to my *good thing!*"

The audience stood to their feet for our recessional as husband and wife. Donna's mother smiled at the audience and leaned into the isle as if to be the first to kiss the bride. What she did instead was to whisper in Donna's ear, "I will never call you Mrs. Kent and I will never acknowledge a child from this relationship!" We were whisked away in a Thunderbird convertible to the reception that was held under a tent in a private front yard. The new friends that we had established were extravagant in their kindness. Food and beverage and cake and music and toasts, and …. I kept looking around for the golden chariot. "Surely, this must be a real life Cinderella rerun," I whispered to my wife. She smiled, trying to ignore the painful echo of her mother's charade.

We didn't have a honeymoon. Her parents were returning two days later so we stayed to honor and entertain them in our home. We spent our last few dollars on mouth-watering groceries for our first meal together. Donna worked all day to prepare her specialty of roast beef and Yorkshire pudding. The meal was a gourmet's delight.

As the head of this new home, I assumed my responsibility and prepared to thank God for his blessings and ask Him to bless the food and our lives. Before we were able to close our eyes, Mother spoke her last words to me. "Well," she announced, "I would like to ask God's blessing but I can't. This is not of God and this marriage will not last!"

Ignoring the statement, I thanked God for His leading and direction in our lives. I committed our marriage and life together to Him, and asked for a safe return journey for our parents. Then I sanctified the meal and the hands that so lovingly prepared it. This was the first time we broke bread together as husband and wife.

Now WOW! - The Anchor Of Faith

Sunny carefree days are filled with hope and faith and joy and laughter. "Lord, this is not one of these days!" Mounting clouds and blowing winds are ominous signs of tough times ahead. It is difficult to maintain hope in the midst of a raging tempest. The continual injections, hip bone marrow biopsies and medication are called therapy. What a misnomer! Therapy is supposed to make one better. Her fatigue is so severe that all she can do is lie quietly and breathe.

The Apostle Paul found himself in a storm of the century. The story is recorded in Acts 27:13-20. *When the south wind blew softly, supposing that they had obtained their desire, putting out to sea ... But not long after, a tempestuous head wind arose ... the ship was caught ... and so were driven. And because we were exceedingly tempest-tossed ...we threw the ship's tackle overboard ...Now when neither sun nor stars appeared for many days, and no small tempest beat on us, <u>all hope that we would be saved was finally given up</u>.* Sound thinking during turbulent times is a rare commodity. The normal reaction is fear. Paralyzing terror! This was clearly underscored by John when he wrote *...fear hath <u>torment</u>.* (1 John 4:18) The Greek word for torment is *kolasis*. It refers to penal infliction, punishment, torture or torment. The Roman Coliseum derives its name from this word.

Faith in defiance of realty is misguided sincerity, but to

overlook the power of God in deference to reality is a mistaken reliance on reason. This conflict between the mind and the spirit will cease only when both are integrated under God. Jesus told us how to do that. He taught a parable ... *that men always ought to pray and not faint* [lose heart]... (Luke 18:1-7) The operative words in this parable are PRAY and FAINT. Two important dynamics are addressed here. The first establishes a spiritual process while the second outlines a psychological dynamic. God has given two powerful resources to overcome trouble. They are the spirit and the mind.

Fainting is the dynamic of the mind. For this reason Paul encourages us to ... *consider him* (Jesus) ... *lest ye be wearied and faint in your <u>minds</u>.* (Hebrews 12:3) Sensory perception is the mind's operating system. It sees only the circumstances that surround it and makes conclusions based on the evidence. Our core beliefs are thus formed. But because the mind is not capable of seeing all the evidence, it is inferior and is often deceptive. There is a big lie in the center of be<u>lie</u>f.

Praying is a function of the spirit. The spirit of man does not operate on sensory perception. It is moved by faith, which is independent of circumstance. The spirit is focused on the promises of God and this leads to hope. *And hope maketh not ashamed* [kataischunoô - confounded, dishonored, disgraced]... (Romans 5:5) Hope then becomes the anchor to the mind during turbulent times. This is clearly pointed out in Hebrews 6:17-19. *Because God wanted to make the unchanging nature of his purpose <u>very clear to the heirs</u>* [we who are born of the Spirit] *of what was <u>promised</u>, he confirmed it with an oath. God did this so that, by two unchangeable things* [God's character and His Word] *in which <u>it is impossible for God to lie</u>, we who have fled to <u>take hold of the hope</u> offered to us may be greatly encouraged. <u>We have this hope</u> as an <u>anchor for the soul</u>, firm and secure.* The word used here for soul is *psuche*. It is frequently translated as mind or soul. Words like psychology, psychiatry and psyche are derived from it.

Peter walked on the water as long as his focus was on Jesus. When he looked at the waves he sank. (Matthew 14:28-30) "Lord, this day I choose to look to you. I instruct my mind to submit to God and His word and come into agreement with my spirit."

Therefore ... let us lay aside every weight, and the sin which so easily ensnares us, and let us run with endurance the race that is set before us, looking unto Jesus, the author and finisher of our faith ... lest you become weary and discouraged in your souls. (Hebrews 12:1-3)

WOW These are WordsOfWisdom we can live by!
><)))*>

A Personal Challenge And Prayer Of Commitment

It has been said that FEAR is an acronym for False Evidence Appearing Real. Don't be daunted by opposition. Never capitulate under the pressure of popular opinion. It is God that you must hear and when He has spoken, you must act upon it regardless of the consequences. The alternative is stagnation. *In thee, O LORD, do I put my trust; let me never be ashamed: deliver me in thy righteousness.* (Psalms 31:1)

"Dear Lord: I shall trust Your Word. Help me to live at peace with all men. Keep my motives ever honorable. Cause me to hear You voice and embolden me to follow your leading. I ask this in the Name of the Son of God, Jesus – Amen!"

Chapter 6

A Marriage Made In Heaven & The Logic Of Faith

The Love Story – A Marriage Made In Heaven

The road that leads to a marriage made in Heaven runs directly through hell. Enamored with each other and our newfound roles, we began life together. Our future prospects looked thrilling and our relationship fulfilling. We were totally complete in each other, but ominous clouds loomed ahead.

An enormous oak tree shaded our front door. It could have been there when the Pilgrims landed in 1620. We could stroll to the Mayflower that was docked a block away. A small kitchen had a table with two chairs. The living room had a sofa and a chair, and the bedroom and bath completed our first home. The owners built the attachment for their mother and when she died, were hesitant to rent it. For some unknown reason, Donna and I found favor in their eyes and they gave us the cottage if I would maintain the garden. "You can have any of the vegetables you wish," she said. What a God send!

Donna worked as head nurse at the Plymouth Hospital. I worked somewhere, anywhere and nowhere. Seven days at a lumber company, one month at a cemetery, four hours in a cranberry bog, all labor intensive and pay deficient. I was well qualified but there was no demand for my services. Every cent we made went to pay back bills. We were hungry.

New England gardens grow profusely. We had tomatoes and corn coming out of their ears! Our diet consisted of bacon, lettuce and tomato sandwiches, stewed tomatoes, tomato soup and tomato whatever! It didn't matter. To us a tomato sandwich and a six-pack of soda was a seven-course meal! One day we went to a local food market. As we pushed the grocery cart down the aisle, Donna began to cry. We had only seven dollars to spend. Putting my arm around her I comforted her, "That's OK honey. It will be different next week." It was. We had only four dollars. I vividly recall that we bought a small aluminum pot. We needed it to prepare, what else, tomatoes! But we had each other, a healthy attitude, our drive, ability and the favor of God to pull us through. And yes, we had plenty of tomatoes that insured our survival.

Donna's sister and her husband pastored the church where we were married, so it was natural that we become involved in church life. We worked together to develope a needed youth ministry. We began to establish healthy friendships and I finally secured a position as a substitute teacher at a Boston high school. Life was sweet, but every day it was turning sweeter.

Late one night the phone awakened us. Donna's mom had a heart attack and was not expected to live. We left immediately. After our twenty-four hour drive we went directly to the hospital. Donna walked into the room and leaned into her oxygen tent. "I'm so sorry my darling. Please forgive me," she whispered and died. Her words were prophetic. She never called Donna as Mrs. Kent and would never need to recognize any children from our marriage. What a needless tragedy! Donna would have made her proud and I would have been the finest son-in-law. However, the Lord was gracious in giving her an opportunity to make peace with her daughter. This she did.

An aging spinster aunt that had a low raspy voice and was hearing impaired, reopened any wounds that may have healed. At the funeral she turned to a person beside her and in a tone that everyone could hear said, "You know, Donna killed her. She died from a broken heart!" I squeezed Donna's hand tightly. After all, I was her "safe place" and she need not respond.

Now WOW! - The Logic Of Faith

A battle wages deep within my soul. I have a profound faith in Jesus, and believe that His Word is as authentic as is His character. And so, I rest my hope and trust in Him. However, I am also a pragmatist and I cannot deny reality. My current situation speaks so loudly that it overpowers God's Word making it almost inaudible. The conflict between my spirit and my mind is fierce. Is there any resolution for this ongoing struggle? Despite our faith and prayer, Donna shows no sign of improvement.

A certain ruler came to Jesus on behalf of his daughter who lay near death. By the time He arrived at his home, the mourners were wailing her demise. "Stand aside," said Jesus, "she is asleep and not dead!" These were the same words Jesus spoke at the grave of Lazarus, whose body was in a state of decay. At this, the people put Jesus to scorn with laughter. The narrative is found in Matthew 9:23-25. *And when Jesus came into the ruler's house, and saw the minstrels and the people making a noise, He said unto them, Give place: for the maid is not dead, but sleepeth. And they laughed him to scorn. But when the people were put forth, he went in, and took her by the hand, and the maid arose.*

What did Jesus mean when He said, "She is asleep?" Was

the maiden taking a nap? Was she in a trance or a coma, or was she indeed dead? The many who came to grieve had examined the evidence and were assured that she indeed was deceased. Forensic science cannot overlook the fact. Reality cannot be denied. The laws of nature are immutable. She was dead! It was for this reason that "they laughed him to scorn!" Faith is not the denial of reality. That is foolish. Faith sees the reality beyond the evidence. Knowing that He is the Resurrection and the Life, Jesus saw a reality beyond death.

In 2006, the newest jumbo A380 Airbus is expected to take off from Toulouse, France. Carrying 820 passengers plus cargo, it will weigh 1,235,000 pounds at take off. Every physics student knows that a heavier than air object cannot fly. A snowflake or feather maybe, but not something exceeding a million pounds! It is the law of gravity that keeps us from falling off the earth. It cannot be denied, negated or annulled. However the manufactures know a law that supersedes the law of gravity. The law that overpowers gravity is the law of aerodynamics.

There is a law in the spirit world that overpowers forensic science. It was this law that Jesus had in mind when He said, *"...the maid is not dead, she sleeps!"* He is the Resurrection and the Life. He has power over life and death, sickness and health, poverty and prosperity. He is God and therefore supersedes all things. *All things were made by him; and without him was not any thing made that was made. In him was life; and the life was the light of men.* (John 1:3-4)

The matter of faith may be wishful thinking to the scientist, a state of denial to the psychologist and unrealistic expectations to the pathologist, but the weight of evidence supports the fact that they who trust in Him shall not be confounded! My mind is focused on another reality, other than the pathologist report. It is a certainty that supersedes fear and sorrow and disappointment and life itself. I know that my Redeemer lives and so I make a rational, quality choice to trust in Him. *Likewise reckon* [logizomai - the words logic, logarithms and logistics are derived from here] *ye also yourselves to be dead indeed unto sin, but alive unto God through Jesus Christ our Lord.* (Romans 6:11)

But without faith it is impossible to please him: for he that cometh to God must believe that he is, and that he is a rewarder of them that diligently seek him. (Hebrews 11:6)

WOW These are **W**ords**O**f**W**isdom we can live by! ><)))*>

A Personal Challenge And Prayer Of Commitment

If a jogger stops for every dog that barks, he will never get to the end of the street. It is also true that if you give up when opposition comes, you will never succeed. Victory comes in the midst of the battle. The cross that Jesus requires us to pick up is not made in the form of a mattress. You live by faith. Keep on keeping on! *Only fear the LORD, and serve him in truth with all your heart: for consider how great things he hath done for you.* (1 Samuel 12:24)

"Dear Lord: Forgive me for thinking of giving up when the cares of this world overpower me. Help me not to become weary and faint in my well doing. Energize me by Your power. Thank You Lord for hearing my earnest plea. I ask this in Jesus Name – Amen!"

Chapter 7

A THANKLESS JOB & THE ABOUNDING FAITH

The Love Story – A Thankless Job

Because Donna's father needed care until he got back on his feet again, we left our beautiful cottage and returned to the home we ran from. Nurses are always in demand so she started work immediately. Our first child arrived ten days before our anniversary and brought much happiness to us, particularly Dad. He was overjoyed. His heart had become soft towards us and he became our most ardent supporter.

A small church needed a pastor and asked me if I would lead the congregation. This was my first "full time senior pastorate." I had made a commitment that I would spend no less than ten hours in research and study preparation for a message. It was the Lord's people and His pulpit, and I was not to be found guilty of feeding His people grain wafers and crackers when His Word was filled with meat. This resulted in a growing church. A restaurant that serves an appetizing meal in a courteous manner will never lack a clientele. Businesses have discovered this to be true.

I became an excellent speaker and taught well. This is what I was called, trained and anointed for. Donna ran the ladies' meeting and the music department. She was an excellent organist and pianist. We became a dynamic duo. The church outgrew the walls, then rented office space across the street, and then expanded next door. But the old guard was not at all pleased with the growth. It threatened their power and authority. "I believe the church should be under one roof," declared an "elected but unregenerate church official!" When asked what we were to do with all the new people, he grunted and said, "I dahknow. Send them away to other churches. We need to go back to things as they was." He didn't know it at the time but his words were prophetic. These were the best five years that church had experienced in its history.

I prepared a series of thirteen messages from the book of Malachi. The theme was a fervent plea to return unto the Lord. *"...A son honors his father, And a servant his master. If then I am the Father, Where is My honor? And if I am a Master, Where is My reverence? Says the LORD of hosts...* (Malachi 1:6) Every week I would give an altar call for response to commitment. There was not a single move. The church was full and the congregation smiled accommodatingly, but not one person stirred. Thirteen weeks went by with no response, until the last sermon of the series. One single person came forward. It was the Pastor! Following the anointed message, I gave the appeal and was so overwhelmed by their hardness of heart that I began to weep. I left the platform and walked to the front of the altar responding to my own altar call. Two weeks later, I resigned.

Our salary was seventy-five dollars a week, and I would frequently need to remind the church treasurer that it was time he paid us. To make up the glaring deficit, Donna worked full time. She also looked after an ever-expanding family and ran her duties at the church. To augment our paltry income, I drove a school bus. Because they had no accommodations for pastoral leadership, they gave us two thousand dollars as a down payment on a house. When we left the church, they demanded full repayment with interest. A sharp real-estate agent that loved us but couldn't tolerate the congregations treatment of us, negotiated a deal on our behalf. Ten dollars a month with no interest until it was paid off! For the next 16 years we faithfully sent them their check of ten dollars. It became a joke to us! By that time, the church had dwindled down to the members of one family; the descendants of the "unregenerate self appointed church official!"

God is no man's debtor! When the last check was sent, we had sufficient money in our banking account to write one check and buy the entire church and property from under them! In the end, they lost everything, possibly their own souls.

Now WOW! - An Abounding Faith

A Miami police report (Associated Press) stated that they arrested a man who robbed two neighborhood banks within twenty minutes, then sat down to rest his tired feet. He told tellers that he had a bomb in his bag. In both cases he asked for and received $100 dollars. Police said that the bag actually contained a can of beer. I surmise that the rest of the six-pack was in his stomach! The bank vault contained multiple millions, but he asked for one hundred dollars. According to his misguided bravado, he got what he asked for.

I smiled as I read the report and marveled at how characteristic this was of our Christian faith. We have faith to swing the small stuff, but healing for a catastrophic illness is over our heads. Asking God to heal an annoying hangnail or a skin rash is so much easier than Acute Leukemia. Believing God for a break through in our finances, or our marriage, or our employment, or our children's welfare is too big a miracle for God to handle! We feel much more comfortable in shallower waters. Asking for things beyond the realm of rational possibility is not within our comfort zone. And so, in similar fashion as the infamous bank robber, we get what we ask for!

Some may confuse presumption or personal desires with faith. Others may see their own misguided imaginations as faith. After all, "God told me," said one person, putting an end to all debate. Who is going to argue with God? Still others have faith in their ability to generate faith; or faith in a circumstance that "it will all turn out OK", or faith in some epiphany or some unexplained sign. Living in a world of delusions is not the same as a faith walk! Despite this abuse, God is pleased to honor faith. And ...*without faith it is impossible to please Him.* (Hebrews 11:6)

The norm for every child of God is an abounding faith. It is often irrational and defies logic. This is the import of Ephesians 3:20. *Now to Him who is able to do <u>exceedingly abundantly above all that we ask or think</u>, according to the power that works in us.* The encouragement that Paul gave the early Colossian Christians was to exercise abounding faith. *As you therefore have received Christ Jesus the Lord, so walk in Him, rooted and built up in Him and <u>established in the faith</u>, as you have been taught, <u>abounding in it</u> with thanksgiving.* (Colossians 2:6-7) The Greek word for abounding is *periseuow,* and it means to super-abound in quantity or quality, to be in excess, superfluous; to excel, to make more and have in abundance enough to spare.

Abraham's example is faith building. God promised this octogenarian that he was going to have a son. His wife Sarah was not far behind in age. The medical odds of this occurring were zero. But faith takes over where the mind stops. *Against all hope, Abraham in hope believed and so became the father of many nations, just as it had been said to him, "So shall your offspring be." Without weakening in his faith, he faced the fact that his body was as good as dead—since he was about a hundred years old—and that Sarah's womb* *was also dead. Yet he did not waver through unbelief regarding the promise of God, but was <u>strengthened in his faith</u> and gave glory to God, being fully persuaded that God had power to do what he had promised!* (Romans 4:18-21)

Thus once again I am renewed in my spirit! And although I'm not skilled to understand what God has willed or what He has planned, this I know at His right hand, stands One who is my Savior! "Yea, living, dying, let me gain my strength, my solace from this Spring, that He who died to be my King, now loves to be my Savior!" We can place our trust in Him. This is abounding faith.

Be anxious for nothing [don't never be worried for nothing no how], *but in everything by prayer and supplication, with thanksgiving, let your requests be made known to God; and the peace of God, <u>which surpasses all understanding</u>, will guard your hearts and minds through Christ Jesus* .(Philippians 4:6-7)

WOW These are **W**ords**O**f**W**isdom we can live by!
>>)))*>

A Personal Challenge And Prayer Of Commitment

The Word makes it plain that they who live by the sword also die by the sword, and what we sow we also reap. Don't sweat the petty things and don't pet the sweaty things. God is no man's debtor. He will honor you according to your faithfulness. *Be not deceived; God is not mocked: for whatsoever a man soweth, that shall he also reap. For he that soweth to his flesh shall of the flesh reap corruption; but he that soweth to the Spirit shall of the Spirit reap life everlasting.* (Galatians 6:7-8)

"Dear Lord: Help me to be faithful to You regardless of the circumstances, and to continue sowing Your truth even when growth is not evident. Help me live in an attitude of positive expectation. Your blessings are without measure. Thank you Lord Jesus for hearing my prayer – Amen!"

Chapter 8

A LATERAL SHIFT & THE SEDUCTION OF FAITH

THE LOVE STORY – A Lateral Shift

I delivered the same series of messages from the Book of Malachi at my next church. Not a Sunday went by that someone didn't respond. What a change in attitude! The incentive was like throwing a steak to a hungry junkyard hound. It is pleasure to feed a hungry baby. This was true not only of our growing family, but also true of God's family. Their eager reception of God's Word engendered our commitment for greater service.

My dedication was noticed by other leaders in our fellowship of churches. I was appointed to head up a "Camp Project" for the denomination. Although I was honored by the appointment, I soon discovered that a title is no more than just that, a title. It was more of a "lateral shift" than a promotion. There was no extra pay, just extra expenses, extra work and more liability. One evening, as I looked at my calendar I discovered that I was going to be away every evening during the month of November. A cold sweat broke across my brow as I realized that I was busy tending other people's gardens, while my own was overgrowing with weeds. Never once did my Precious complain, but she looked so tired. Her work now was with the provincial government setting up homes for the mentally handicapped. In addition to this, she carried full responsibilities at the church. By now we had three children and the fourth on the way. Our Pediatrician took me aside one day and asked, "Wilf, do you know what is causing all these pregnancies?"

I determined to take regular time for nothing and no one but my family. This did not make me a popular chap because the misguided expectation of a leader is total subservience to the will of the people. My first responsibility however, was to my wife and children. "What I am doing, is not God's will. It is other people's will," I thought. Furthermore, a growing discontent fermented within my heart. I witnessed the glaring inconsistency between what we believed and what we experienced. There was as much immorality among church-going people as there was in the secular world. We used a euphemism to deaden the embarrassment and called it "sexual indiscretion!" Theft and embezzlement we called "financial misappropriation" and church fights we called "business meetings". Garbage dumps were now called "land fills", but they bred the same vermin and smelled just as badly.

As much as we loved God's Word and the ministry to which God called us, we became tired of "religiosity", "churchianity" and the spiritual lingo called "Christianees". We had made friends that were to last a lifetime, but knew that God had something else for us. After five years of fruitful ministry, we resigned.

Donna secured a position as director of nursing at a large nursing home, and a university gave me a very favorable transfer of credits towards my master degree in psychology. We secured our visas, sold all our possessions, packed what we could in two cars, picked up our four kids and left for the USA.

Sadly, I was not a pleasant or patient husband during that time. I entertained bitterness and worry over our treatment at the church, and transferred my frustration to my wife. She was always the gracious peacemaker and every disagreement ended with me groveling at her feet in contrition. Our disagreements never lasted but a few hours. Major differences lasted a little longer and all our warfare ended in a truce before bedtime. I can recall only a few times that we allowed the "sun to go down on our wrath."

Now WOW! - The Seduction Of Faith

Numerous Bible verses adorn the walls of her hospital room. A collection of promises regarding healing, affirmations of victory, declarations of hope, emails pledging prayer and support, and get-well cards greet her each time she is able to open her eyes. In the quiet hours I read them and ask, "Is that for us? Can I apply that verse to our situation? Was that written for a specific time or can it apply to the present? Am I doctrinally correct in claiming that promise? Is it out of context? Did God really mean that for me? Truly, hath God said?" Sounds familiar doesn't it?

Yea, hath God said? This was the lie that plunged mankind into the abyss of sin and sickness and poverty and estrangement from God. *Now the serpent was more crafty than any of the wild animals the LORD God had made. He said to the woman, "Did God really say, 'You must not eat from any tree in the garden'?"* (Genesis 3:1) Now I find myself asking the same question.

As a young man I dedicated myself to study the Word to insure doctrinal correctness. False doctrine obscures the truth and has led many astray. So I enrolled in the finest theological schools and studied a curriculum that included Hermeneutics, Theology, Ethnology, Eschatology, Ecclesiology, Doctrine, Church History, Greek and more. After five years of formal study, I graduated with my degree in Theology and the ability to *"rightly divide the Word of truth!"* (2 Timothy 2:15) But now my years of training plague my mind. I stare at the walls covered with the promises of God and question whether they fit within parameters of accurate interpretation. "Is it good exegesis to claim these promises? Is that verse for now or was that fulfilled?" Hath God really said?" Privately, I wonder if my questions are any different from that of the serpent?

Good doctrine is essential, but *"The just shall live by faith!"* (Romans 1:17) I can live without theology and exegesis or Greek and still please God, but I cannot please Him without faith! *But without faith it is impossible to please Him.* (Hebrews 11:6) Isaiah asks a poignant question. *Who has believed our report? And to whom has the arm of the LORD been revealed* [made strong]? (Isaiah 53:1) Despite the many signs performed by Jesus, the Jewish leaders refused to have faith in Him as Messiah. John stresses this in John 12:37-38 when he writes the following account. *But although He had done so many signs before them, they did not believe in Him, that the word of Isaiah the prophet might be fulfilled, which he spoke: Lord, who has believed our report? And to whom has the arm of the LORD been revealed?"* To whom is the arm of the Lord revealed? The answer is unmistakably clear. The Lord will bare His arm on behalf of those that believe His report. What moves the hand of God is simple faith that what He has promised, He is also able to perform. Personal virtue, exact exegesis and sound doctrine are noble, but they can be counter-productive when they interfere with faith! We can "ace" the entire theological curriculum and still wander in the desert of unclaimed promises!

A fresh understanding of faith reinvigorates me. I determine that my theology will no longer hijack my faith in Him. I will not allow my understanding to seduce my faith in Jesus and His promises. The Children of Israel wandered forty years in the wilderness because they chose to believe the "evil report" brought to Moses by ten of the twelve spies.

Because they did not believe the Lord's report, they all died in the wilderness. Joshua and Caleb however, believed the report of the Lord, and [they] quieted the people before Moses, and said, *Let us go up at once and take possession, for we are well able to overcome it. (Numbers 13-14)* God honored their faith and strengthened His arm on their behalf to enter the Promised Land!

Forty years later, at eighty-five years of age Caleb gives us this testimony. *As yet I am as strong this day as on the day that Moses sent me; just as my strength was then, so now is my strength for war, both for going out and for coming in. Now therefore, give me this mountain of which the LORD spoke in that day...* (Joshua 14:11-12)

WOW These are **W**ords**O**f**W**isdom we can live by!
><)))*>

A Personal Challenge And Prayer Of Commitment

The Christian walk is much like the tides of the ocean. When the tide is in, the waters come right to the forefront. The relaxing view is unobstructed and stretches off into the horizon. When the tide is out, it exposes all the mire, debris and sludge that lie beneath the surface. Don't be alarmed by your carnal nature. God is dealing with that, and will complete the task before your graduation. Just continue to feed the spirit. *This I say then, Walk in the Spirit, and ye shall not fulfil the lust of the flesh.* (Galatians 5:16)

"Dear Lord: I am sorry for the times that my flesh shows so strongly. Help me to walk in Your Spirit. Live in and through me. May my behavior never bring shame to Your name. I ask this in Jesus Name – Amen!"

Chapter 9

BE QUIET AND GO TO SLEEP &
THE AMBIVALENCE OF FAITH

THE LOVE STORY – Shut Up And Go To Sleep

I drove a mini Morris, an English car that resembled a roller skate with headlights. The inside was stuffed full to the ceiling with kids toys, kitchenware and personal items. Three bicycles and other playground equipment that were roped together, protruded from under the trunk lid that could not be closed. Donna followed in an American sized car and had the children. It was over packed with our clothing and personal items. When we presented our immigration papers to the US Customs Agent at the border, he just shook his head, stamped our papers and waved us on!

I too was shaking my head. "I must be nuts! What am I doing, uprooting my family and moving to Who Knows Where, and for what reason? How am I going to support my family? Going back to school at 34? That's is absurd," I thought. As the miles stretched before us, I began to wonder if we would ever get there. "Poor Donna," I mused. "She has all the kids. I wonder how she is holding up? They must be driving her nuts!" It was the safest car and offered the greatest protection, so we agreed to this. We worked out a sign language so we could communicate. If Donna flicked on her headlights, I knew we had to stop. When she flicked them repeatedly, the need was urgent.

For the first few months we lived in two rooms among the construction debris of the nursing home. The accommodations included the cement floor, exposed wires, open ceiling, no running water and a pail for potty purposes. Donna bathed the children outside with a garden hose. They thought it was a real hoot! Other adjectives frequently came to our minds. We had an icebox that kept the milk cold, a two-burner hot plate and bed sheets that covered the windows at night. For a city girl, this was really roughing it! To make things worse, I had a week of speaking engagements and abandoned her there alone. That was such a thoughtless thing to do. Upon returning, I promised never to put opportunity ahead of responsibility like that again.

One of the nursing home owners had a house he was trying to sell and arranged a mortgage with one of his banker friends on our behalf. He saw this as his opportunity to "unload" his slow moving property. For us, it became an opportunity of a lifetime. We moved from the construction debris of a half completed structure into our own home. This was to become our first home in the country we adopted, and the beginning of an exciting journey! We were able to buy furniture on a payment plan based on the strength of Donna's position and salary. The only employment I could find was at a rubber tire factory. A main ingredient in tires is carbon, a black dust-like substance that permeates everything. I would come home with only the whites of my eyes and teeth showing. I looked like one of my Black Brothers. Following a quick shower and a change of clothes, I was off to university for a five-hour stint.

Each day was a grinding schedule. I dressed the children, fed them and got them ready for school in the morning. Then I was off to the factory from 8 through 4. By that time Donna was home with the children for the evening. I had one hour to come home from the factory, clean up and get to class at five where I struggled to pay attention until 10. Then I had to drive home and do my assignments. The torture started the next day at 6 a.m.

It was the hardest time of our marriage, but we knew that it was temporary. It was also the sweetest, and one that offered us the greatest opportunity and blessings. Furthermore, one cannot grow a garden or mine gold without digging. "This is our garden, Sweetheart. We have to dig it. I love you so much," I whispered in her ear. "Be quiet and go to sleep. I love you too," she responded! I knew that. I had no doubt that she loved me. She had demonstrated that so well in so many ways.

Now WOW! - The Ambivalence Of Faith

Yesterday the sun shone. Hope filled the air. Positive expectation was everywhere. Donna was scheduled to come home. Her first treatment was over. But that was yesterday! The doctor's report quickly overcast the sky and dampened the enthusiasm. Pulmonary emboli (blood clots in both lungs) confine her to complete bed rest until they could be dissolved. "You're not going home for a while," he said. King David writes of his ambivalent emotions. When I felt secure, I said, *"I will never be shaken!" O LORD, when you favored me, you made my mountain stand firm; but when you hid your face, I was dismayed* [baw-hal' meaning troubled, alarmed, agitated]. (Psalms 30:6-7)

The Beetles popularized a disappointing sentiment with their hit song <u>Yesterday</u>. "Yesterday, All my troubles seemed so far away, Now it looks as though they're here to stay, Oh, I believe in yesterday!" Three times King David laments his woes with these words, *Why are you cast down, O my soul? And why are you disquieted within me?* (Psalms 42:5; 11, 43:5)

The Bible records many great men of God that have temporarily lost their grip on the anchorage of faith. Elijah overpowered Ahab's false prophets with resounding victory. The next day he fled into the wilderness for fear, sat under a tree and prayed that God would kill him. (1 Kings 19:1-4). Jonah preached a great revival in the pagan city of Nineveh. He then sat in the shade *and wished death for himself, and said, "It is better for me to die than to live.* (Jonah 4:5-8) Moses lamented that God chose him to "baby-sit" his murmuring people. And King David frequently lodged his complaint to God. But He quickly identified the problem and prescribed the cure. *Why are you cast down, O my soul?* The problem is always the soul [mind]. All it sees is the destruction that wastes at noonday and the terror by night, and it melts in fear. Then David commands his soul to refocus its vision! *"Put your hope in God, for I will yet praise him, my Savior and my God."*

A study of Jehoshaphat's response to severe stress (2 Chronicles 20:1-22) is a telling example of how every child of God can find victory in the midst of trial. He faced an innumerable army in which it was impossible for him to win. Destruction was a certainty. When he saw the size of the army that came against him, he melted in fear. Fear! Fear is a common response to potentially harmful situations, but note the steps that led him to victory.

1. He Retreats To God - V3b
2. He Regrouped His Resources - V4-5
3. He Remembered God's Power - V6
4. He Rehearsed His Great Past - V7-8
5. He Reassures Himself Of God's Promises - V9
6. He Reviews The Facts - V10-11
7. He Refocuses His Perception - V12
8. He Renews His Commitment - V13
9. He Revitalizes His Courage - V14-15

10. He Reestablishes His Position - V16-17
11. He Responds With Praise & Worship - V18-19
12. He Is Renewed With Courage - V20
13. He Is Reinforced With Song - V21
14. He Is Rewarded With Victory - V22

To you, O LORD, I called; to the Lord I cried for mercy: "What gain is there in my destruction, in my going down into the pit? Will the dust praise you? Will it proclaim your faithfulness? Hear, O LORD, and be merciful to me; O LORD, be my help." You turned my wailing into dancing; you removed my sackcloth and clothed me with joy, that my heart may sing to you and not be silent. O LORD my God, I will give you thanks forever. (Psalms 30:8-12)

WOW These are WordsOfWisdom we can live by! ><)))*>

A Personal Challenge And Prayer Of Commitment

Take comfort in the fact that He is always, fully aware of your needs and is ever present to walk you through your most difficult times. The name Jehoshaphat, is a contraction of two words; *Jehovah*, the name for God, and *Shaphat* meaning rule, ruler or judge. It literally means, "God is Ruler", "God Rules" and/or "God is Judge. God was his rule and judge. ... *be content with such things as you have. For He Himself has said, "I will never leave you nor forsake you." So we may boldly say: "The Lord is my helper; I will not fear. What can man do to me?* (Hebrews 13:5-6)

"Dear Lord: Help me to follow the example that Jehoshaphat left for me. I ask for Your rule in my life. Be my judge. Help me to focus my eyes on You. I ask this in Jesus Name – Amen!"

Chapter 10

I Hate This Job & The Words Of Faith

The Love Story – I Hate This Job

I can't handle this any longer! My back hurts. I'm sick. I think I have a fever. I can't go to the tire factory today," I complained to Donna. I could hear her footsteps approaching me, and the familiar sound of the nurse's snap, snap, snap as she shook down the thermometer. "You're not sick. You better get to work," she ordered. "But if my temp goes up, I'm liable to damage my brain." "You had brain damage when I married you!" We both laughed, I kissed her and off I went. How we enjoyed our playful trysts. Regardless of the hardship, we could find something to laugh about.

Work at the factory and school however, was no laughing matter to me. I hated the job! I hated the road that led to the factory. I began to hate the car that took me to the factory. Of some two thousand employees, I was among the best educated yet my job title was "Broom Sweeper and Utility Gopher". At least that is what it should have been. In my mind it was a loathsome, demeaning job. Day after day after day it was SOT, Same Old Thing. I hated the job! In order to get through to graduation in the shortest amount of time, I stacked my classes to run concurrently without a break, both summer and winter. The classes were not that difficult. The assignments were laborious. Yard work around our new home was pleasant. The moments we shared together as a family were Heavenly. Work at the tire factory was a nightmare. And did I mention that I hated the job? Sadly, the pressures began to effect me as I rebelled against my circumstances. "The church, the move, the school and now this," I grumbled.

One winter's day I took my lunch break and walked down the railroad track that was lined with boxcars laden with carbon and rubber and whatever. I found an empty car and crawled inside. Pulling the door shut to insure that I was alone, I pushed my face into the corner and began to cry. "Why Lord? All these years in school and for what? For this? Is this what your plan is for my life? I can't handle it any longer. If I had brain damage at least I would be happy. Now I have to face this intolerable hassle with my full wits intact."

There was no audible voice or blinding epiphany, but I knew that God was talking with me. "Where were you when I created the universe and hung it upon nothing? Where were you when I set a boundary upon the ocean and said, 'Hither to shalt thou come and no further?' Where were you when I called you and ordained you before I formed you in your mother's womb?" My crying turned from self-pity to humble repentance. At that moment I had a major attitude alteration. "I'm sorry Lord. Please forgive me for my obstinate resistance to Your will. If You choose to keep me here, by Your help I will make the best employee they have ever had." I am convinced that Heaven's host of angels erupted into song, "Hallelujah!"

My thirty-minute encounter with the Lord was transforming. It was "Broom Sweeper and Utility Gopher" that crawled into that boxcar, but what sprang out was the "Superintendent of Sweeping Services!" Same job, same broom, same old thing but now there was a new person at the end of the handle. And yes, I still hated the job but now it was in the Lord's hands. Two weeks later the factory went on strike. Rather that walking a picket line, I applied for work elsewhere and became a caseworker and psychologist for a children's home.

I didn't attend the graduation services. I asked the University to forward my degree by mail. When it arrived, I filed it away in my desk. Somehow, it was too painful to display it. I never went back to the factory or the school. I just kept going and never looked back. My wife was glad to get her husband back and the kids were happy to have Daddy home again.

Now WOW! - The Words Of Faith

"How is your wife," asked a well-meaning shopper? "She came through her chemotherapy very …" Before I was able to complete my sentence she interrupted, "Let me tell you about my dad. His chemotherapy left him so sick with sores that he never recovered! So we are praying for Donna." "That's too bad, but thank you for asking", I said quietly. At the checkout a kindly checker asked, "How is Donna doing?" I told her that she responded remarkably well to the chemotherapy. "The next step is the bone marrow transplant", she informed me. "My sister's transplant didn't take and she died." "Thank you for asking", I whispered. My strength quickly drained. A pall hung over my head as I struggled to carry the few bags of groceries to my car. I sat motionless pondering what had just happened. I knew that they were well meaning but I was far better off without their concern. I regretted that I had ever talked with them. Why would I have reacted so strongly to their words? They were words, just harmless words.

The power that a word can unleash is enormous. God formed the universe by the power of His <u>word</u>. *We understand that the worlds were framed by the <u>word</u> of God*

(Hebrews 11:3) Jesus is called the Word in John 1:1-3, by whom and through whom the universe was created. *In the beginning was the Word, and the Word was with God, and the Word was God ...Through him all things were made; without him nothing was made that has been made.*

Words are not harmless! They contain blessing and cursing, life and death. This was Solomon's observation. *Death and life are in the power of the tongue...*(Proverbs 18:21) Balak, King of Moab hired Balaam, a prophet of God to curse Israel. (Numbers 23:13-23) Several words are translated as curse. They all carry a similar meaning: curse, vilify, bless, salute, blaspheme, express, name, pierce, appoint, swear and adjure. All these are all dispatched by the tongue! James 3:5-9 declares that the tongue is a fire, a world of iniquity. *The tongue is so set among our members that it defiles the whole body, and sets on fire the course of nature; and it is set on fire by hell... no man can tame the tongue. It is an unruly evil, full of deadly poison...*Unwittingly spoken by well meaning people, words that amounted to curses were uttered. Willingly I received them.

Jesus warned us about the serious nature of idle talk. *But I say to you that for every idle word men may speak, they will give account of it in the day of judgment. For by your words you will be justified, and by your words you will be condemned.* (Matthew 12:36-37) The Apostle Paul challenged the Ephesians with these words, *Do not let any unwholesome talk come out of your mouths, but only what is helpful for building others up according to their needs, that it may benefit those who listen.* (Ephesians 4:29) It was for this reason that King David prayed, *set a guard, O LORD, over my mouth; Keep watch over the door of my lips.* (Psalms 141:3)

The words that were spoken at the supermarket may have been true, but it served only to disquiet my heart. Then I remembered the portion that the Lord had given me before this sad saga began. *A good man ... will never be shaken... He will not be afraid of evil tidings; His heart is steadfast, trusting in the LORD. His heart is established; He will not be afraid, Until he sees his desire upon his enemies.* (Psalms 112:5-8) I made a quality choice to listen to the words spoken by God and not man. Then they cried out to the LORD in their trouble, And He saved them out of their distresses. He sent His word and healed them, And delivered them from their destructions. (Psalms 107:20)

My son, give attention to my words; Incline your ear to my sayings. Do not let them depart from your eyes; Keep them in the midst of your heart; For they are life to those who find them, And health to all their flesh. (Proverbs 4:20-22)

WOW These are **W**ords**O**f**W**isdom we can live by! ><)))*>

A Personal Challenge And Prayer Of Commitment

Hardships are never pleasant, but neither are they permanent. Everything has an end. Following that, there is a new beginning. If God is leading you, then beyond your difficult present, there is a significant future. *Thou therefore endure hardness, as a good soldier of Jesus Christ.* (2 Timothy 2:3)

"Dear Lord: Forgive me for my complaining and my irritable disposition. Help me to trust in Your leading even when the way seems bleak. I commit my future into Your hands and by Your help, will endure hardness as a good soldier. I ask this in Jesus Name – Amen!"

Chapter 11

WALKING IN DIVINE FAVOR & THE AIDS OF FAITH

THE LOVE STORY – Walking In Divine Favour

Throughout our lives we yearned for more of God. During the tough times we leaned on Him heavily, trusting Him for our next meal. Our desire to know Him better never waned even though things were getting much easier now. Surely, there must be more to this thing called Christianity than what we had experienced. God is without limit, and we knew that we hadn't arrived. Donna had acquired a prestigious position with the State. Her role was to assess the programs of State Hospitals and develop a curriculum for staff development. This required her to travel. I was busy as well. Along with being the Academic Dean of a small Bible School, I developed a Drug and Rehab Center with the Rescue Mission. All the while, I was slowly building my own private counseling practice. We were both familiar with hard work so everything seemed a challenge. None of our responsibilities at home or work was neglected. Life was sweet. We were always well aware of God's divine favor, but now were beginning to enjoy it. Still we had a hunger for spiritual growth.

We sold our first home and built a new one. Two years later we sold that and built a larger home in an upscale part of the city. Because of our work, we became known throughout the State. Donna was in demand as a speaker and taught everything from neighborhood Bible classes, to Women's Conferences to Mayor's Prayer Breakfasts. She was honored by being listed in <u>Community Leaders and Noteworthy Americans</u> by the American Biographical Institute. I was in demand as a seminar lecturer and conference speaker. Our friends were many. God had taken us out of a dark corner and set us in the light. Still the hunger to know Him better continued.

One day Donna was invited to speak at a Women's Event, a two-hour drive from our home. The evening's program included the husbands and I was asked to join them. On our drive, Donna said, "The men will be there. Just for fun, why don't we do something together? Let's do something on marriage." We had never spoken in tandem before, but the idea sounded captivating. Hurriedly we jotted down a few points that we wanted to cover, agreed to give deference to and support each other, and go for it. When Donna was introduced, to their surprise we both got up. We had no notes so we were not bound by preconditions. The dialogue flowed so naturally and left such an impact on the audience that soon invitations began to come from all parts of the world. Because of the requests for three and four day seminars, we had to develop a curriculum resource material. It included thirty-six classes titled <u>The Exciting Marriage</u>. We could not have orchestrated this. There was no doubt that this was God's doing.

For the next twenty years we would move among the finest churches in most denominations and visited many countries that included Canada, Belize, Mexico, England, Poland, South Africa, Singapore, Malaysia, Israel and yes, the USA. At first we limited our seminars to one per month because of our responsibilities at home. As the children grew older, the schedule was increased.

Everything we did, we did together. We were colleagues, lovers and best friends. It was a pleasure to work on the platform together. Even our fights were enjoyable! There was never any rancor, duplicity, bitterness or competitive posturing. She was my servant, and I was hers. And although ours was a "fairy-tale marriage", we had a deepening desire for the Lord. Perhaps this was the reason for our blissful relationship. The answer came in a most unusual way.

Now WOW! - The Words Of Faith

As devotees of Jesus, we have benefited greatly from our brothers and sisters in the Body of Christ. The many cards, letters and emails, the evening meals, financial help and phone calls have served to engender our faith. Couples from South Africa, Canada and California have offered to come and stay with us during therapy. Friends from thirty years past drove three thousand miles to encourage us, pray with us and celebrate communion, only to turn around a few hours later and drive the two-day journey home. An eleven year old girl sent Donna a card telling her that she loved her and included tithe from her allowance, two one-dollar bills. We have never experienced such extravagant demonstrations of love. What encouragement to faith. We shall be forever grateful.

Faith may begin as a theological concept but it is activated by action. It is the "doing" that sets faith into motion. The scriptures makes this clear in Philippians 4:9. *The things which you learned and received and heard and seen in me, these __DO__, and the God of peace will be with you.* The "believing" part is much easier than the "doing" in that it is passive. Believing is the simple act of agreeing to a notion. It can be a mere mental acquiescence to a concept. Doing however, is burdensome in that it requires motivation and action. This often requires encouragement, particularly when it comes to faith.

As members of the same body (Romans 12), we are instructed to care for one another, and encourage each other in the things pertaining to faith. This was Paul's exhortation to the early Hebrew Christians. *And let us consider one another in order to <u>stir up</u> love and good works, not forsaking the assembling of ourselves together, as is the manner of some, but <u>exhorting</u> one another, and so much the more as you see the Day approaching.* (Hebrews 10:24-25) The original word translated as "stir up" means to come along side and sharpen, or to provoke into action. To "exhort" means to invoke, implore, beseech or entreat. Sports teams, sales groups and the armed forces know the importance of such briefings. Often called pep talks or rallies, the meetings are used to instruct, encourage and motivate. Members leave these assemblies so hyped with confidence that they feel they could "lick the world single handedly!" The Apostle Paul warned us not to use ... *any unwholesome talk ... but only what is helpful for building others up according to their needs, that it may benefit those who listen.* (Ephesians 4:29)

How does one stimulate faith in someone else? By offering, "If there is anything I can do to help, just ask?" No! That places the needy person in the role of a supplicant, and the one that offers in a position of control. I determined never to humiliate a needy person by putting him in a position of a beggar. A better suggestion is to say, "Here, let me help you!" But how do I help someone if I don't know where it is that he needs help? That is where we need to be sensitive to the Holy Spirit. Since we are members of the same body of which Jesus Christ is the Head, is it not reasonable to think that the Head will inform the body where the need is? Let the Holy Spirit tell you how you are to help in word or deed. Then do it without invitation! *Let the word of Christ dwell in you richly in all wisdom, teaching and admonishing one another in psalms and hymns and spiritual songs, singing with grace in your hearts to the Lord.* (Colossians 3:16)

It is my belief that Christians are coming under increasing attack from the enemy. To avoid standing alone against demonic forces, we need to become an active part of a prayer and Bible study group, home cell, church or some accountability-support system, particularly *as you see the Day approaching.* (Hebrews 10:24-25) Furthermore, it is imperative to have a workable knowledge of who we are in Christ Jesus, what He purchased for us on Calvary, and what faith in God and His Word is, if victory is to be ours. *So then faith comes by hearing, and hearing by the word of God.* (Romans 10:17)

As you therefore have received Christ Jesus the Lord, so walk in Him, rooted and built up in Him and established in the faith, as you have been taught, abounding in it with thanksgiving. (Colossians 2:6-7)

WOW These are **W**ords**O**f**W**isdom we can live by! ><)))*>

A Personal Challenge And Prayer Of Commitment

It takes two to make a happy marriage. A miserable disposition, an inflexible attitude and an "unteachable" spirit always result in an adversarial relationship. In a society that advocates self-promotion, gentleness and servitude is seen as weakness. To the contrary, it is a sign of great strength and results in cooperation, efficiency and happiness. *Your love must be without hypocrisy. Abhor what is evil; cling to what is good. Be devoted to each other with mutual affection. Excel in showing respect for each other. Never be lazy in showing such devotion. Be on fire with the Spirit. Serve the Lord. Be joyful in hope, patient in trouble, and persistent in prayer ... Rejoice with those who are rejoicing. Cry with those who are crying. Live in harmony with each other. Do not be arrogant, but associate with humble people. Do not think that you are wiser than you really are. Do not pay anyone back with evil for the evil he does to you. Instead, focus your thoughts on what is right in the sight of all people ... Do not take revenge, dear friends, but leave room for God's wrath ... Do not be conquered by evil, but conquer evil with good.* (Romans 12:9-21)

"Dear Lord: This is the kind of person I choose to be. Forgive me of my self-centeredness and help me to be "Jesus" to others, particularly those of my own family. I ask this in Jesus Name – Amen!"

Chapter 12

STINKING HIPPIES & THE AIDS OF FAITH

THE LOVE STORY - Stinking Hippies

My Ph.D. dissertation was titled <u>Factors Leading To Drug Abuse And The Rehabilitation Of The Drug Abuser</u>. The study required original research and statistical documentation, so I associated myself with a Hippy community. I grew a beard and a mustache, dawned a muumuu (loose shirt), shorts and flip-flops, and went "grooving" with a clipboard under my arm. What a joke! If I thought that I was going to blend in with the crowd, I was badly mistaken. I was immediately identified as bogus, so I had no alternative but to reveal my true purpose. I offered my services as a counselor one night a week. They appreciated my honesty and accepted me as a "brother ".

On my second visit someone said, "We understand you know something about the Bible. Will you give us a Bible rap?" I assumed what they wanted was rapport about the Bible, so I said, "You bring your friends next Monday evening, and I will tell you all you want to know about the Bible." I was astonished at what happened. There sitting on the floor were some three hundred hippies from all walks of life, from all ages and in varying stages of withdrawal. The small room was so crowded, that I had room enough to shift my weight from one foot to the other. I could not see the back wall because of the marijuana smoke. Reaching for a drink and a hairy arm grabbed it from me, "You don't want to drink that, Man," he said. "If you do, you'll be flying for a week!" Come to think about it, I always felt good after the teaching sessions.

I spoke for an hour and twenty minutes, as the smoke dissipated. I had never seen such hunger or been given such respect by any group. This began a relationship that lasted almost two years. One summer, 400 hippies responded to Jesus and were baptized. I did not lead any of them to the Lord, nor did I baptize them. They did this among themselves. All I did was to teach the word.

One day someone suggested that we have a prayer meeting before the study. I thought this was a good idea and agreed. That evening about ten or fifteen people gathered. They were on the floor as usual. One young Jewish lady raised her hands above her head and with tears running down her face thanked God that she discovered Jesus as her Messiah. Then something tragic happened. Unbeknown to anyone including herself, she began to pray in a language no one understood. I immediately surmised that this was not of God and was about to censure her when the Spirit of God spoke to me and said, "Wilf! Be quiet. None of this is your doing. You are merely a teacher!" The effect on the entire group was remarkable. It spread like wild fire, and soon I found myself standing on the outside periphery of the inside circle.

God had given the hippies what we had been searching for all our lives, but neither Donna nor I wanted that! After all, my theology condemned those that had a "prayer language". Like the elder brother of the prodigal son, I became envious. "Lord, all my life I have served you. I have been faithful to you and have endured many hardships for your name's sake. I am upright and loyal, and you give them what rightly belongs to me? They are just a bunch of bearded stinking Hippies. I can't turn my nose off! Why would you give Your Spirit in such an abundant measure to them and not to me?"

On my knees I renounced my religiosity and asked God to make me a hippy. Several weeks later I experienced the fullness of the Holy Spirit. Donna did too, but some time later. Our hunger for Him was being satisfied.

Now WOW! - The Boldness Of Faith

The Oncologist peered over his glasses and said, "So, what we have here is some good news and some bad. You are in remission. Although we cannot find any blast cells in your system, we know that they are still there. We recommend that you enter a second phase of chemotherapy. It is equally as invasive as was the first. When you recover from that, we will talk about bone-marrow or stem-cell transplant." "Remission ... but we know that the blast cells are still there?" "This is the voice of faith in science" I thought, "and it generally ends in death!" If I should declare the promises of God with the same confidence, I would be guilty of presumption or wishful thinking at best. It is true that they who refuse to accept the inevitable live in a world of denial. And yet, faith in God is not a denial of reality. Furthermore, the contrary is often true. Confidence in the medical arts alone can lead to the denial of God with devastating consequences.

Asa, a righteous King of Israel is a case in point. He renewed the altars of Jehovah and called upon the Lord. Among his many reforms, he dispatched teachers of the Word into all the provinces. During the later part of his life he developed a severe illness in his feet. *And <u>because he sought the physicians and not the Lord, he died</u>.* ... Asa *became diseased in his feet, and his malady was severe; yet in his disease he did not seek the LORD, but the physicians. So Asa rested with his fathers; he died in the forty-first year of his reign.* (2 Chronicles 16:12-14)

So emboldened with faith, we determined to face the future trusting in God's promises! But what if? What if I boldly declare my faith in the One who is able to heal, and then she dies anyway? Won't that prove the unbeliever's opinion that Christians' are an unrealistic lot? Will it not shake our faith in God and His Word? With so much intercession on our behalf, will it not impugn the character of God? Furthermore, will not our declaration of faith be seen as mere presumption?

To avoid such an embarrassing "faith shattering" possibility, many Christians opt for a less threatening and timid faith, and pray, "Lord, if it is Your will…" This becomes a theological backdoor where we allow God to do His sovereign thing despite our earnest desire. After all, He is God! That way, one's faith is preserved whether one lives or dies. It is a benign way to express a faith that places no demands on our prayer or the Lord. Everyone benefits from this spiritual safety net except the one that truly needs it.

One cannot read the history of the early church without realizing the universal and ubiquitous nature of faith. It operated everywhere and though every believer. The Gospels record many miracles. After His resurrection, Jesus gave His powers to His followers. *Behold, I give you the authority to trample on serpents and scorpions, and over all the power of the enemy, and nothing shall by any means hurt you.* (Luke 10:19) *So Jesus said to them again, "Peace to you! As the Father has sent Me, I also send you."* (John 20:21) *But you shall receive power when the Holy Spirit has come upon you* …(Acts 1:8) *And these signs will follow those who believe: In My name they will cast out demons; they will speak with new tongues; they will take up serpents;*

and if they drink anything deadly, it will by no means hurt them; they will lay hands on the sick, and they will recover." (Mark 16:17) Peter and John healed the lame man at the gate Beautiful. (Acts 3:1-8) With great power the apostles witnessed (Acts 4:33), performing many signs and wonders. (Acts 5:12) Stephan, full of faith and power, did great wonders and miracles (Acts 6:8). Persecution scattered the believers and they preached the word everywhere. (Acts 8) Philip healed, preached and cast out demons. Peter healed Aeneas and raised Tabitha from the dead (Acts 9:33-40). The supernatural power of the Christian faith was evident everywhere and multitudes turned to Jesus! The result of such a witness was the exponential growth of the church. They turned the world upside down!

What has changed? Certainly not the Lord! *Jesus Christ is the same yesterday, today, and forever!* (Hebrews 13:8) What has changed is our lack of boldness to trust the Lord for the miraculous. We have lost our unique distinction of the supernatural! A miracle is not an expected phenomenon for most Christians. Because the church no longer displays the supernatural, we wield no more influence that any civic organization. We have become irrelevant. I for one, will believe that God delights to move His sovereign hand on our behalf and in answer to our petitions that we desire of Him. And so regardless of the outcome, we continue to trust in the Lord and power of His might.

Now this is the confidence that we have in Him, that if we ask anything according to His will, He hears us. And if we know that He hears us, whatever we ask, we know that we have the petitions that we have asked of Him. (1 John 5:14-15)

WOW These are WordsOfWisdom we can live by!
><)))*>

A Personal Challenge And Prayer Of Commitment

All that God requires of you is your hunger for Him. Correct doctrine, faithfulness in service and a holy walk is important. It identifies you as a devotee of Jesus, but all this can be a religious or academic exercise. Only a hunger for Jesus can satisfy your soul. Sounds like a paradox, doesn't it? But it is true. Jesus made this clear when He said ... *Blessed are they which do hunger and thirst after righteousness: for they shall be filled.* (Mathew 5:6)

Dear Lord: Here is my cup Lord. I lift it up Lord. Come and fill this thirsting of my soul. Bread of Heaven, feed me till I want no more. And make me whole. In Jesus Name – Amen!

Chapter 12

EZ STREET & THE FOOLISHNESS OF FAITH

LOVE STORY - EZ Street

The prospects look very bright. My private counseling practice had grown so well that Donna was able to quit her government job. For the first time she was able to be a stay-at-home mom. This was welcomed news to the children who were entering their teen years.

She volunteered her service as a camp nurse and organist for a large church. The Camp provided us with fully furnished accommodations in a mobile home near the lake. It was an ideal location that offered privacy with a commanding view. Donna's duties were light. She spent most of her day lounging in a lawn chair in the shade of oak trees that overlooked a lake, reading her books. Birds would serenade her in the morning with their singing. A gentle breeze stirred the leaves as if to greet her awakening. Chipmunks came every morning for their meal of crackers that she would feed them. Even the fish swim near the dock in anticipation of her coming. Because everyone ate at the dining room, her housework was reduced to the bare necessities. Had we arrived in Heaven? The children and I thought so.

All during the summer months, I would drive from my

office to spend the evening with my wife and family. Because the office was closed from Friday afternoon through Monday afternoon, it had the effect of a long weekend. We used these times to conduct seminars during the fall and spring seasons. June through August is off-time for most churches, so the demand for seminars died each summer. This provided an ideal setup for the Kent family.

We had finally arrived on easy street. Without question, this was the better side of God's divine favors. The practice continued to grow and I was looking for property to build my own clinic. We had become friends with the owner of the city's largest construction company, and he offered to build and finance the project at cost plus ten percent. What an opportunity! We had a large two-story brick home that backed onto virgin timber. A Ford LTD and a Lincoln Town Car were parked in our garage. We never strove for wealth or fame, neither did we take credit for anything we had. We had been faithful to the Lord and content with little, and now we had much. Contentment is not dependent upon the abundance of the things one possesses, however we discovered that it was a lot easier to be content with much!

Some of our former friends that visited us from our previous churches, became annoyed with our affluence and found it their duty to lecture us on the subject of materialism. They didn't take into account our sacrifice and the many years of hardship, study and self-denial that we had put into what we had. All they could see was the consequence of our labors as compared to the results of their apathy. Solomon declared that ...*The blessing of the LORD, it maketh rich, and he addeth no sorrow with it.* (Proverbs 10:22) We discovered however, that God's blessings worked in cooperation with personal industry, and the harder we worked, the more of God's blessings we experienced. *Yet a little sleep, a little slumber, a little folding of the hands to sleep: So shall thy poverty come as one that travelleth; and thy want as an armed man.* (Proverbs 24:33-34) We had friends, respect, security, a profession and ministry. There was not any need to move from our spot. We had established roots and things could only get better.

One day we received an invitation from a mega-church in the "Deep South" to do a weeklong marriage seminar. The response was overwhelming, and we were pressed upon to move our headquarters there. "Not again! We don't need to move anywhere. We have just arrived at the place that were had strived for. We have it made here. Our roots have taken hold," I argued. Moving meant closing down a lucrative practice, selling our home and going back into uncertainty.

The offer did seem tempting nonetheless. "If I could get seven patients within the first month, I think we can make it," I said. "We have walked by faith all our lives. Let's go for it," encouraged Donna. It was David that declared ... *they trusted in thee, and were not confounded.* (Psalms 22:5) Within one month we were gone. And yes, rather than having seven patients within the first month, I had thirty-five.

Now WOW! - The Foolishness Of Faith

We were so sure, so full of faith. There was not a single question in our minds but that the bone-marrow biopsy would disclose no cancer cells. Sadly, the report revealed that her system was filled with blast cells with only a 10-20% chance of survival with immediate chemo-therapy. We were stunned into silence! A heavy pall filled the car as we drove home. Not a word was spoken for the longest time. To lighten the overwhelming burden, I looked at my wife and said, "Well, I've got you today, Babe", but that offered little comfort to either of us.

For the first time we were forced to face the dismal probability of death. When we got home we fell into each other's arms and wept. How precious are the memories we have gleaned over the past 44 years! Holding her closely, I caressed her face. How gentle was our embrace, how tender our touch as hot tears coursed down our faces. It all seemed like yesterday that we first met. "Lord, don't let it end now!"

Questions flooded my mind. What went wrong? Were we foolish to have faith for healing? Was praying for a miracle folly? All the prayers, the verses pinned to the hospital walls, the positive testimony to the medical staff, was that for naught? Was our hope misguided foolishness? And what of the examples from scripture? Was David ill-advised when he penned ... *Bless the LORD, O my soul, And forget not <u>all</u> His benefits: Who forgives <u>all</u> your iniquities, Who heals <u>all</u> your diseases, Who redeems your life from destruction, Who crowns you with lovingkindness and tender mercies, Who satisfies your mouth with good things, So that your youth is renewed like the eagle's.* (Psalms 103:1-5) Was Job hasty when in his agony he declared, *Though He slay me, yet will I trust Him.* (Job 13:15) Is faith synonymous with foolishness?

To the natural mind, faith is foolishness. Faith is foolish in that it pierces through the natural to touch the supernatural. It is not confined to limitations of natural phenomenon. Faith focuses its vision on God and His promises, and because the mind cannot see the supernatural, it concludes that faith is foolish. Paul the Apostle makes it clear that to the natural man, faith is foolish. *The man without the Spirit does not accept the things that come from the Spirit of God, for they are foolishness to him, and he cannot understand them, because they are spiritually discerned* [understood or comprehended]. (1 Corinthians 2:14) The original word used here for the <u>natural man</u> is *psuchikos*. It is a contraction of two words meaning: mortal soul, and the physical or bestial nature. Words like psyche, psychology and psychometrics are derived from it. It well describes man's natural instincts and observations. To such a mind, any benefit that Jesus won for us on the cross of Calvary is sheer absurdity.

For the message of the cross is foolishness to those who are perishing, but to us who are being saved it is the power of God. (1 Corinthians 1:18)

Having faith in God's ability and delight to perform miracles on behalf of those that seek Him, is hardly foolishness. On the contrary, *"to us who are being saved it is the power of God."* (1 Corinthians 1:18) So then confidently we choose to live by the "foolishness of faith!" *For we walk by faith, not by sight ... Therefore we make it our aim, whether present or absent, to be well pleasing to Him.* (2 Corinthians 5:7-9) As long as He gives us breath, we shall love Him and serve Him, and expect the supernatural as our daily lifestyle.

But God chose the foolish things of the world to shame the wise; God chose the weak things of the world to shame the strong. He chose the lowly things of this world and the despised things—and the things that are not—to nullify the things that are, so that no one may boast before him. It is because of him that you are in Christ Jesus, who has become for us wisdom from God—that is, our righteousness, holiness and redemption. Therefore, as it is written: "Let him who boasts boast in the Lord. (1 Corinthians 1:27-31)

WOW These are WordsOfWisdom we can live by!
><)))*>

A Personal Challenge:

The main factor that must be considered in every decision is the will of God. Security, provisions, guarantees, insurances, these and many more are important. But if you have all these and you are out of His will, you will never find contentment. *Let your conversation be without covetousness; and be content with such things as ye have: for he hath said, I will never leave thee, nor forsake thee.* (Hebrews 13:5)

Dear Lord: You will never leave me nor forsake me. I am fully secure in my knowledge of You. Direct me in my motivation and the application of my abilities. I pray this in Jesus Name – Amen!

Chapter 14

FROM EZ STREET TO BIG TIME & THE WAIT OF FAITH

LOVE STORY – From EZ Street To Big Time

Rather than creating a lull in our lives, the move catapulted us into success. During one of our Marriage Seminars a stranger sat in the front row protecting a brief case. "Who is that man," I asked the Pastor? "I don't know. I have never seen him before," he answered. He came to every meeting and listened intently. Following the five-night seminar, he approached us carrying his brief case and requested a private interview. I was curious as to what he was protecting and hoped it wasn't a shotgun! Turning to Donna I whispered, "I don't think we were that bad, were we?" She just smiled.

When he opened his case it revealed several cameras and the portfolios of well-known ministries. He was authentic and substantiated everything he said with evidence. "I am a promotion agent," he said. Throwing the promotional photos of various people on the table before us he continued, "I made these people. No one heard of them when I came to them. I can make you both a household word. You have a unique style of ministry, one that leaves a rich deposit in the lives of people. It will cost you 30% of all that you make, but the 70% that will be yours will be far beyond anything that you can imagine. I guarantee that Your names will be a household word!" Then he pushed a contract toward us and asked us to take it home and read it.

You can understand out elation! This was an opportunity to move off EZ Street into the Big Time! During the several days that followed we talked about the possibilities and opportunities. Our minds swooned with excitement, but as we talked further, a clearer picture began to slowly immerge. Our goal was to promote God's Word and bring maturity to the body of Christ. His singular goal was to promote us. We began to question the promotional gimmicks he might use to promote us. Will his advertising methods be compatible with our way of presentation or will he seek to change what we do? Furthermore, is what we are tempted to do, God's will? There could be no question that what we had accomplished this far was His doing. Why change it? So we prayerfully considered our dilemma.

One day while in quiet meditation, I could hear my thoughts explode in my head. Promotion comes from the Lord not a "flesh-peddler!" Quickly I turned to Psalms 75:6-7 and read the following admonition. *For promotion cometh neither from the east, nor from the west, nor from the south. But God is the judge: he putteth down one, and setteth up another.* Both Donna and I agreed that we heard from the Lord. The next day I phone the agent and said, "Thank you so much for considering us and presenting us with your fine offer. At this time, we do not feel that we are ready for such a venture."

We never did become a "household word". The masses never heard the Dynamic Duo known as Wilf and Donna Kent. That was a big price to pay for nonentity. Or was it? Is it not He who directs the steps of upright people? Is it not the Holy Spirit who guides us into all truth? Yes indeed. So we put the offer out of our minds and settled into my private counseling practice and week-end ministries. Our seminars however, continued to expand and we found ourselves spending more time on tour than we did in our office. Ministry doors were opening everywhere. We did not ask for speaking opportunities or for financial support, neither did we develop promotional materials. All the way, our Savior led us!

Now WOW! - The Wait Of Faith

The house remains dark and uninviting. There are no colorfully wrapped gifts under the Christmas tree this year, and the stockings that were hung on the mantle with care, are empty. Room 2317, Porter Hospital, has become our home and I sit endless hours by her bedside seeking to bring encouragement and comfort. In my private moments of weakness I ponder our fate, "How long must we wait? The fall is long past, the New Year is here and still we wait! Months have passed and there are no answers. How long Oh Lord, must we endure?" To validate my agony I quote the Psalmist, King David. *My soul is in anguish. How long, O LORD, how long? Turn, O LORD, and deliver me; save me because of your unfailing love.* (Psalms 6:3-4) Despite our keen disappointment, I have never heard her complain or ask "God, why?" She has never felt sorry for herself, never displayed anger at her circumstance and has never lost hope. "This in not my wife" I think, "This indeed is a handmaiden of the Lord!" And I determine to treat her with the dignity that she deserves.

Our children and their families gathered in the hospital lounge on Christmas day. Donna gained sufficient strength to come down the hall to the lounge. The hospital had wheeled in a piano for her at her request. It was in perfect tune. A number of the patients and staff came when Donna began to play Christmas carols. Soon, the place was filled as music drifted down the halls beckoning the weary. It became a Christmas worship service! After the carols were sung, Donna stood and briefly challenged the audience. After hundreds of public appearances, this was to be her last. Following the service, our children laid hands on their mother and prayed for her healing. Other patients asked to be included. What a ministry!

It was then I remembered Paul's circumstances. He was in jail, chained to a Roman guard and on trial for his life. The smells that surrounded him did not come from "chestnuts roasting on an open fireplace"! His dark and damp confines reeked of body odor, sewage and the stench of sickness. It was in this adverse setting that he penned these words of encouragement. *But I would ye should understand, brethren, that the things which happened unto me have fallen out rather unto the <u>furtherance</u> of the gospel.* (Philippians 1:12) The word translated as "furtherance" is *prokopay*, a first century reference to a workforce that went before the army to clear away the overburden of rocks, trees and anything that might hinder the soldiers' advancement. Paul viewed his circumstances as "bush-whackers and rubbish-clearers" that made a road for the advancement of God's Word into the palaces and governmental offices of Rome. There can be no doubt that Donna's illness was the entry of the Christmas story to the staff at the hospital.

Quickly our focus shifted from our own personal disappointment to the opportunities that our circumstances provided. The colorful lights that deck the houses, the Christmas tree adorned with decorations, the gifts beautifully wrapped and carefully placed on display, the sounds of laughter and conversation, the smell of baked goodies and foods of all varieties that are so essential for family reunions, diminished into drab insignificance when compared to the peace that comes to a tear-stained face of a grieving soul. One woman in her forties shared how she lost her mother and father within the last few months, and now

Comfort In Times of Grief

---

her husband is down the hall from our room. I took her hand and prayed for comfort, encouragement and healing to her husband. That evening, she pushed her cot beside his bed and fell soundly asleep.

No, we don't want to be here at 2317 and earnestly pray that the Lord will hear our cry and deliver us healthy and strong. Sickness and disease have been indicted and condemned by God. It has no right in our body and we give it no authority to stay there. We have no formulae for healing, no exacting ritual that we follow and no unique mantra that we recite. We simply claim His word and commit our future to Him. In the meantime, let us wake every morning to speak the goodness of His name, until we close our eyes in sleep again.

Rejoice evermore. Pray without ceasing. In every thing give thanks: for this is the will of God in Christ Jesus concerning you. Quench not the Spirit. Despise not prophesyings. Prove all things; hold fast that which is good. Abstain from all appearance of evil. (1 Thessalonians 5:16-22)

WOW   These are **W**ords**O**f**W**isdom we can live by!
><)))*>

A Personal Challenge And Prayer Of Commitment

It is not God's intent that His children walk in darkness. He has promised to direct your steps. Acknowledge Him. Act upon His promptings. His word is without error and can be trusted. *A man's heart deviseth his way: but the LORD directeth his steps.* (Proverbs 16:9)

Dear Lord: Help me to hear Your voice. Speak to me and give me the strength to obey. I pray this in Jesus Name – Amen!

Chapter 15

PAIN IN THE GRASS & THE WAIT OF FAITH

LOVE STORY – Pain In The Grass

Life would be wonderful if weren't for teenagers. Our four darling children suddenly turned into monsters. Their characteristics resembled that of Frankenstein and Godzilla more than that of Wilf and Donna. The room of our eldest "dearest daughter" looked like an explosion is a lingerie factory. "Clean up this 'pigsty'. Your mother is not your house maid," I would demand. A packrat by genetics, our second "dearest daughter" brought home everything from stray ferrets to bird's nests. "Your room looks like a storage shed for the neighborhood garage sale. Clean it up," I chided. Our "dearest son" always had his stereo cranked up to 12 on a 10-decibel dial. My entire body would start to pulsate with the base rhythm the moment I stepped from my car onto the driveway. "Shut that thing off! You're driving me insane. And did you mow the lawn like I asked?" "I guess I have to do that myself," I thought. "What a pain in the grass!" And our youngest "dearest daughter", Miss Priss, as she was called by her siblings, was always seeking the center of attention. "Look at what I can do," she would proclaim, and then proceed to dance and jump around the house. "Sheesh! I think insanity is hereditary and I am convinced that parents get it from their teenagers," I muse quietly.

Things began to change quickly. One of our daughters got married and with her went all her storage stuff. Another daughter went off to college, taking her car and most of what she owned. Our son went off to private school. Within a two-week period we lost 75% of our family.

I recall the day I came home from the office and there was no music to greet me. I could actually make it into the house without losing my balance! Going upstairs to our son' room, I looked around at the things left behind. Then I went over to stereo and turned it on. Yep, it still worked. How I wish he were home so I could hear his noise again. I then walked into our daughter's room. It was empty. Even the bird's nests were gone. Everything flew the coop! The third room was clean, almost sterile. There were no wet towels on the floor or nylon hose hanging over the shower curtain rod. The bed was made. A few of her clothes hung in the closet.

For a moment I stood in stunned silence, then burst into sobbing. To that point my Donna had never seen me cry. But that day was different. I wept like a baby as I suddenly realized that those years were gone forever. All we had left were the pictures, videos, audiocassettes and the memories of what it used to be. How I wished we could have them back again. I longed for the opportunity to get impatient with their brief and passing idiosyncrasies, just one more time. But it was over, and with its passing we crossed into another time zone.

Together we sat on the sofa in each other's arms as she tried to console me. I, ever the strong one, was the vulnerable one now and she now became my safe place. Neither one of us had dreamed that the 'empty nest' would seem so utterly empty. All of a sudden our parenting skills were not in demand. We were no longer needed as disciplinarians or guardians or instructors or coaches. We were now needed as friends. It was a role that we had to learn.

As the years stretched out before us, we discovered the meaning of King David's words ...*sons are a heritage from the LORD, children a reward from him. Like arrows in the hands of a warrior are sons born in one's youth. Blessed is the man whose quiver is full of them. They will not be put to shame when they contend with their enemies in the gate.* (Psalms 127:3-5)

Now WOW! - The Peace Of Faith

I watch her sleep soundly and free of pain. The shadows lengthen as I stare out the window and watch a full moon rise slowly into a blackening sky. "This is the third full moon I have seen from this window," I think to myself. Moons have long passed but it seems like yesterday that we received the devastating news.

I struggle to find meaning and purpose for our ordeal but only unanswered questions come to mind. Why should one with so much to offer be set-aside at the height of her productivity? Why, with so much prayer offered to God on our behalf, is she still sick? If God is for us, why then is there so much against us? Introspectively, I question what sin I may have committed to hinder His blessing? Then I question whether my questioning is of any value. Everything has become an incomprehensible riddle with no defining points of reference. Perhaps it has something to do with the fact that God's ways are not man's ways. *For my thoughts are not your thoughts, neither are your ways my ways, saith the LORD. For as the heavens are higher than the earth, so are my ways higher than your ways, and my thoughts than your thoughts.* (Isaiah 55:8-9)

The most baffling of all questions has to do with the peace and assurance that we both experience. How is it that when we find ourselves facing the greatest challenge of our lives, we are flooded with an inexplicable calm? We share moments of tears and sorrow, but the overriding emotion is peace. Our anxious thoughts are brief. We have no fear. There is no anger toward God or at circumstances. There has never been a moment of regret and we refuse to entertain self-pity. That too, has something to do with God! He has promised ... *As your days, so shall your strength be.* (Deuteronomy 33:25)

Shadrach, Meshach, and Abednego were confronted by a devastating challenge. King Nebuchadnezzar erected a heathen statue and commanded that everyone bow in worship to it. The punishment for refusal was death. When they refused, a furnace was heated seven times hotter than normal for their incineration. Their testimony is faith engendering. They...*replied to the king, "O Nebuchadnezzar, we do not need to defend ourselves before you in this matter. If we are thrown into the blazing furnace, the God we serve is able to save us from it, and he will rescue us from your hand, O king. But even if he does not, we want you to know, O king, that we will not serve your gods or worship the image of gold you have set up."* (Daniel 3:16-18) They refused to bow! They did not bend or buckle, nor did they burn!

We are confident that God is able to deliver us from this ordeal, and it is to this end that we continue to pray. *We will not forget ALL of His benefits towards us ... Who forgiveth all thine (our) iniquities; who healeth all thy (our) diseases; Who redeemeth thy (our) life from destruction; who crowneth thee (us) with lovingkindness and tender mercies; Who satisfieth thy (our) mouth with good things; so that thy (our) youth is renewed like the eagle's.* (Psalms 103:2-5) However, if He chooses not to, be it known that we shall not succumb to the enemy's tactics neither will we march to his drum beat. By God's help, we reiterate the words of Joshua, ... *as for as for me and my house, we will serve the LORD.* (Joshua 24:15)

Nebuchadnezzar discovered a fourth man in the flames!

He answered and said, Lo, I see four men loose, walking in the midst of the fire, and they have no hurt; and the form of the fourth is like the Son of God ... *Then Shadrach, Meshach, and Abednego, came forth of the midst of the fire... upon whose bodies the fire had no power, nor was an hair of their head singed, neither were their coats changed, nor the smell of fire had passed on them.* (Daniel 3:25-27) There is a third Man in our relationship. Because He is able to deliver us, there isn't anything that the three of us cannot do!

Now unto him that is able to do exceeding abundantly above all that we ask or think, according to the power that worketh in us, Unto him be glory in the church by Christ Jesus throughout all ages, world without end. Amen. (Ephesians 3:20)

WOW *These are WordsOfWisdom we can live by!*
><)))*>

Personal Challenge And Prayer Of Commitment

Time is a thin slice that is wedged in between the past and the future. It is called NOW. It's passing is instant and if you are not alert you will miss it. Enjoy each moment that the Lord grants you. *See then that ye walk circumspectly,* (exactly, diligently, looking carefully around) *not as fools, but as wise, Redeeming* (buy up, ransoming; rescuing from loss) *the time, because the days are evil.* (Ephesians 5:15-16)

"Dear Lord: Help me to stay balanced when things disappointment me. Help me to overlook the petty things. Give me the ability to enjoy the good things the present has to offer. I pray this in Your Name, Jesus – Amen!"

Chapter 16

A Love Letter To God & The Risk Of Faith

Love Story – A Love Letter To God

It was a habit of mine to write my thoughts down on paper. During my college days it was important to keep notes on each lecture. As a pastor, my sermon notes served as guideposts that directed me through the maze of exegesis, hermeneutics, soteriology, angelology, eschatology, theology and more. As a therapist, my profession required it. Hence it became second nature for me to document any poignant thought by pen.

One day I sat at my desk and wrote a love letter to God. It went something like this: "Dear Lord. You have been so good to me. I have walked in Your divine favor all my life and I give You thanks. You have given me health, recognition, honor, wealth and a wonderful wife and family. You have supplied all my needs. You have been extravagant in Your provision and I don't need or want anything. Thank You Lord!" I sat in quiet contemplation, savoring my good fortune. Then I added one further thought. "P.S. Lord. There is something I do want. I want to know You better. As a matter of fact, I would give You everything I own to know you better." Then I had the audacity to sign it. We frequently stood in church to worship and piously sang, "Take my life and let it be, consecrated Lord to thee. Take my silver and my gold, not a mite would I withhold!" Let me give you a word of advice. Don't sing it!

Our seven-year wilderness began with the loss of our Lincolns, then the ranch and rental properties and finally our home. While away on one of our seminars, our son called and said, "Dad, you have been evicted from your home. You have three days to move out or they will seize your furniture." An investment with someone whom I trusted implicitly, left me destitute. In our absence, our children packed us up and moved us into a rental home. Except for our household and personal effects, we had lost all our assets. To make things worse, because we had recently moved to a new city, I also lost any recognition that I had earned. No longer was I known as Dr. Kent, the respected psychologist. I was now Wilf what? It became apparent that this was the title that was to remain with me throughout the rest of my life.

To complicate things even further, I didn't hear the voice of God for seven years. Night after night, I pled with God asking for some sign, instruction, correction, anything that would indicate He still acknowledged my presence. Nothing. The enemy came at me to convince me that I had committed the unpardonable sin. Although I racked my brain, I could not think what it might be. So I confessed all my known sins once again. Then I confessed things that might be sins. I confessed things that I should have done but didn't. I even confessed other people's sins, but found no response from Heaven. Completely stripped of everything important to me, I felt abandoned by God. Except for my precious Donna, I was left destitute.

Rummaging through dust-laden boxes that had now been stored for several years, I ran across a hand written letter that looked familiar. It read, "Dear Lord. You have been so good to me ...You have been extravagant in Your provision and I don't need or want anything ... P.S. Lord. There is something I do want. I want to know You better. As a matter of fact, I would give You everything I own to know You better." I began to cry and laugh at the same time as God spoke to me through my own handwriting! His silence was broken.

Now WOW! - The Risk Of Faith

Expecting a miracle is a hazardous pursuit. Risk is an inherent quality of faith. Because the outcome can never be predicted, faith has a high level of uncertainty. To many, faith and presumption are synonymous. "Am I living in denial to expect divine intervention in my situation" I wonder? "Will my testimony to the healing power of God seem irrational if she doesn't survive?" I can hear them whispering, "He's a nice man, but a bit misguided by such wishful thinking." And for fear of ridicule, I am tempted to succumb to unbelief, terrified to step out in faith and believe God lest I fall on my face in disgrace.

The entire Jewish race was in peril of genocide under the despotic plans of Haman the Agagite. Queen Ester placed her life at enormous risk when she approached King Ahasuerus uninvited. She had no assurance that he would spare her life. ... *I go in unto the king, which is not according to the law: and if I perish, I perish.* (Esther 4:16) She disclosed that she was a Jewess and that her race was in jeopardy. The result was that the Jewish Nation was spared. Was that faith or presumption?

Jonathan and his armor bearer had no guarantee that God would deliver the entire Philistine army into their hands when they climbed to their stronghold. Furthermore, they were not altogether certain that God had commanded them to do so. And Jonathan said to the young man that bare his armour, *Come, and let us go over unto the garrison of these uncircumcised: it may be that the LORD will work for us:*

for there is no restraint to the LORD to save by many or by few. (1 Samuel 14:1-23) Was that reckless bravado or was that faith?

David ran toward the nine-foot giant named Goliath, armed only with a sling and a stone. *Thy servant slew both the lion and the bear: and this uncircumcised Philistine shall be as one of them...* (1 Samuel 17:36) That was not teenage idealism. Each example underscores the fact that faith is superior to overwhelming odds of fact.

And then there is Moses "almighty". *So the LORD said to Moses: See, I have made you as God to Pharaoh ...* (Exodus 7:1) He was specifically instructed to go to Pharaoh and demand, "Let my people go!" When he hesitated, God promised to go with him. But note the perplexing guarantee that God would always be present. And God said, *I will be with you. And this will be the sign to you that it is I who have sent you: When you have brought the people out of Egypt, you-will worship God on this mountain.* (Exodus 3:12) The sign of God's presence will come after the fact! "After you have taken the risk of confronting Pharaoh and enduring the potential humiliation, torture, imprisonment and possible execution, you will know that I was with you when you worship me in this mountain!" To Moses, God's promise of His presence appears as proof posthumous! The risk of obeying God was terrifying! Remember that Moses was a fugitive from justice and wanted for murder. He was a traitor to the Pharaoh and his country. Herding cattle for forty years in this wilderness didn't given him much opportunity to hone his verbal skills. Furthermore, his resources consisted of his tunic, sandals and a staff. Alternatively, the Pharaoh's of Egypt were worshipped as gods and they held the power of life and death. The uncertainty of his task was daunting, but he believed God and entered the arena of world history

Most people want irrefutable assurances before exercising faith. Tangible proof like Gideon's wet and dry "fleece of wool" (Judges 6), a vision or dream, some extra-terrestrial visitation or an earth shaking epiphany would be an incentive for faith. Not so! What we believe in this scenario is our sensory experience and not the Word of God. He that runs the risk of faith in God is not plagued with self-doubt and anxious fear. Believe God and "lay it on the line!" "Lord, help me to be that person!"

... it pleased God through the foolishness of the message preached to save those who believe ... to the Jews a stumbling block and to the Greeks foolishness, <u>but to those who are called ... Christ</u> [is] <u>the power of God and the wisdom of God</u>. Because the foolishness of God is wiser than men, and the weakness of God is stronger than men. (1 Corinthians 1:21-25)

WOW These are **W**ords**O**f**W**isdom we can live by!
><)))*>

Personal Challenge And Prayer Of Commitment

The blessings of God are not always appreciated. That is because His blessings often come in the form of trouble. Rarely is trouble seen as beneficial, but it is in the midst of trial that God's genius is woven. Here He strengthens our metal, engenders our resolve and refines our character. *Wherein ye greatly rejoice, though now for a season, if need be, ye are in heaviness through manifold temptations: That the trial of your faith, being much more precious than of gold that perisheth, though it be tried with fire, might be found unto praise and honour and glory at the appearing of Jesus Christ:* (1 Peter 1:6-7)

"Dear Lord: Help me to see the broader picture. Work Your perfect will in my life. I pray this in Jesus Name – Amen!"

Chapter 17

THROUGH THE WILDERNESS BAREFOOTED & THE LIBERTY OF FAITH

LOVE STORY – **Through The Wilderness Barefooted**

I would rather be tied naked to a pole in the town's square and flogged with a chain, than to go through that experience again. For seven long years we wandered through a wilderness with no direction, encouragement or visible means of support. This was particularly difficult for Donna. Her nest was completely disrupted and dismantled. The security and affluence that we had worked so hard to gain was now all gone. During this time, she never lost grip on the anchorage of faith. Only once did she question as to whether God actually cared, and that only briefly. Never once did she chide me for my poor investment, even though she had begged me a dozen times not to get involved. Her strength of character and personal resolve was exceeded only by her grace and gentleness and trust in God. What a saint!

A friend of mine gave me a computer. "You need to learn how to use one of these things," he said abruptly. He set it up in a basement room, gave me a few instructions and left. "Thanks," I muttered. At first I would come down into the room and look at it from behind the door. I guess I had a fear that it might byte. Later I had the nerve to turn it on. It didn't! I began to type my resource materials and became fascinated with what it could do. It then became a challenge and then a pleasure. I discovered my penchant for words and ability to arrange complex concepts in simple terms. Soon Donna began to call me the "Cellar Dweller".

I began to spend more and more time in the "Lower Level". From the darkness of a basement room and the depths of our despair, a new couple and ministry immerged. A curriculum of thirty-three university level courses were written and accredited, eight books were published and resource materials on personal growth, marriage and family relationships in abundance. Churches and colleges began to incorporate course material into their schools. The demand for materials became greater than one person could handle. Soon we were more in demand than ever before.

One New Year's Watch-night Service, the pastor of our church asked the audience for testimonies. "Give God the glory for what He has done in your life over the past decade. Tell us about His leading in your life," he said. People were quick to share the blessings of God. Some had family members that came to Jesus, others were healed of severe illnesses and still others gave God praise for a new job, a new car, a new house or an addition to their family. Donna and I sat quietly holding hands but said nothing. It was a faith building service.

One week later, as we were driving down an interstate highway, I looked at Donna and asked, "Do you remember the New-Year's Watch-night Service? What came to your mind as the greatest blessing over the past decade?" We both looked forward in stone silence, as if afraid to look at each other. Tears coursed down our faces as we realized that the greatest blessing was the wilderness that we had just walked through in bare feet. It was here that we learned of His abiding presence. He never left us. He never forsook us. He was there all the time! In retrospect we both thanked God that He found us sufficiently faithful to test us. And with that realization, we never looked back. We had every confidence that He who kept us from falling would continue to do so well into the future.

For the next twenty years we would travel the world teaching God's principles of victorious Christian living. We never asked for support. We didn't have any health or accident insurance. We had no pledge of income from any source. God was our supply! We had learned to trust Him for that and discovered that He is no man's debtor.

Now WOW! - The Liberty Of Faith

Daily I make my petition known to Him who hears our prayers. "Lord, I call upon You in my distress. My soul is in torment. Turn not Your ear from me! Hear me oh Lord, and deliver me!" Despite my earnest pleading, the heavens are as brazen brass and the only response I hear is the echo of my plaintive plea. Every day I hope that tomorrow will be a better day, but each morning dawns with my expectations shattered by hurt and disappointment. Then I remember the words from my high school English Literature class, "Tomorrow, and tomorrow, and tomorrow creeps in this petty pace of time from day to day, and all our yesterdays have lighted fools the way to dusty death." – William Shakespeare. Sad is the dilemma that recalls Job's lamentation, *For the thing I greatly feared has come upon me, and what I dreaded has happened to me.* (Job 3:25)

I hate it! But it is not the apparent silence that I abhor. He is always here. He has promised NEVER to leave me nor forsake me, and in my moments of grief I sense His comforting presence and hear His still small voice. It is my obsessive fixation with the problem that offends me. It dominates my every thought. Every conversation, every activity and each event is filtered through the grid work of my own self-absorption. I have become a prisoner of my own preoccupation. This is what I hate!

The unexpected and distasteful visits every person at some time in life, and the normal human reaction is the same. David, the Psalmist wrestled with a similar fixation when he questioned, *Why art thou cast down, <u>O my soul</u>? and why art thou disquieted in me?* (Psalms 42:5a) The problem is always the mind. It can see only part of the picture and its senses can never extend beyond the reach of the fingers tips. How can the finite understand the Infinite? It can't! It's the "thinker" (mind) and the "feeler" (emotions) that must be brought under His control. When one chooses to park in the quagmire of despair, the outcome is a *"disquieted soul"*. David refused to dwell here. He continued by giving us the solution to his dilemma, ... *hope thou in God: for I shall yet praise him for the help of his countenance.* (Psalms 42:5b) Hallelujah!

My critics far outnumber my supporters. "What about your faith? If you really had faith, you wouldn't be in this predicament!" "God's judgment comes upon the disobedient. Repent and all will be well!" "Your theology is warped and your exegesis misguided. You can't apply that passage to your situation." "You base your hope on things out of context!" "You must follow this formula for healing; eat these kinds of foods; buy this life changing supplement; listen to these tapes; read this book; come to hear this speaker and above all ..." Most are well intended and offer good advice that should be followed. However, at this present moment, I can qualify only under the "Simplicity Clause!" *Then called I upon the name of the LORD ... <u>The LORD preserveth the simple</u>: I was brought low, and he helped me. <u>Return unto thy rest, O my soul</u>; for the LORD hath dealt bountifully with thee. For thou hast delivered my soul from death, mine eyes from tears, and my feet from falling.* (Psalms 116:4-8)

During my difficult time I command my mind to anchor onto God's unchanging Word. In doing so, an unexplainable peace and freedom floods my soul as I hear Him say, *I will never leave nor forsake you* (Hebrews 13:5), *I will never allow more trial than you are able to bear* (1 Corinthians 10:13), *as your day, so shall your strength be* (Deuteronomy 33:25). In this we are resolute, that in life or in death we will praise Him.

... *Blessed is the man who fears the LORD, Who delights greatly in His commandments ... Surely he will never be shaken; The righteous will be in everlasting remembrance. He will not be afraid of evil tidings; His heart is steadfast, trusting in the LORD. His heart is established; He will not be afraid, Until he sees his desire upon his enemies.* (Psalms 112:1-9)

WOW These are **W**ords**O**f**W**isdom we can live by! ><)))*>

A Personal Challenge:

God is not through with us yet. God's testing periods were never designed to punish you. All punishment for our sin was nailed to Calvary. The trials of your faith are put in place as "training seminars" for your growth and well-being. *No discipline seems pleasant at the time, but painful. Later on, however, it produces a harvest of righteousness and peace for those who have been trained by it. Therefore, strengthen your feeble arms and weak knees. "Make level paths for your feet," so that the lame may not be disabled, but rather healed.* (Hebrews 12:11-13)

"Dear Lord: It hurts so much! Help me learn my lesson well and quickly, so that I may graduate soon. Reluctantly but willingly, I submit my future to you. I pray this in Jesus Name – Amen!"

Chapter 18

GUESS WHAT HAPPENED & THE FLUCTUATION OF FAITH

LOVE STORY – Guess What Happened

We went from place to place together and worked jointly on the platform as a team. Although I enjoyed golfing, when I had four hours to spare, I couldn't think of anyone I would rather spend that time with than my Donna. She was my co-worker, partner, lover and best friend. We were never apart from each other and had no occasion to ask, "Guess what happened?" We were both there when whatever happened, happened!

Our goal was to make a contribution to the lives we touched. Personal contact is more effective than a lecture series in reaching people. We therefore chose to stay among the people to whom we were ministering. When in the Black or Colored locations in Africa, we slept in their homes. Among the East Indian population of South Africa, the peoples of Singapore and Malaysia, the First Nation People of Canada and the vast cross-section of the Caucasian population, we broke bread together and slept in their homes as well as ministered to them. One group came to us and said, "When white people come to minister to us, they always go back to the big city to stay in their hotels. You are the first white people to eat and sleep with us!" We considered it an honor to be invited into their homes.

The result of this choice was both exciting and challenging. In every case, we were treated to the best they had. There were times that our accommodations included a thatched-roofed cottage with an on-suite bath and maid services. We had no trouble adjusting to that. Sometimes it consisted of a mattress in a humid room that had no kitchenware or cutlery with which to eat our food. For one full week we stayed in a room that served as a kennel for a dog. Each morning the displaced dog would scratch at the door trying to get in. On one occasion our room was so small that the both of us could not stand upright together. Donna had to enter and crawl into bed. Then I would follow. The child's bed was the size and thickness of a postage stamp! Never did we see our ministry as "Suffering for Jesus!" It was an adventure that we would repeat year after year. The stories that have accumulated over twenty years of travel can fill a book.

Regardless of the uncertainties and hardships that we may have faced that day, we could always retire for the night in each other's arms. "This is my favorite time of day," I would whisper in her ear. Somehow, being together made us complete. Every other concern drifted off into insignificance. We were together and that made the trials of the day worth it. Furthermore, we knew that we were walking in His divine favor.

One particular day our 1000-mile trip took us through a warring faction, where the previous day's uprising killed several people. As we neared our destination we drove to the police station to inquire the status of the road ahead. "I dah know. Go see," was the official response. Everything we had was in our car. With a violent carjacking that took place every 28 minutes, we were prime targets. As we approached what looked like a militia, we pulled off to one side of the road and asked the Lord for wisdom. Should we go forward or should we drive the distance back to safety? After a moment, we decided to continue and ask God for His protection. We approached the armed men and slowly meandered through the maze of tanks and other assorted armored vehicles. Somehow we had become invisible. Although we were close enough to touch them, I don't think anyone noticed us. That evening as we retired for the night, we could hear the rattle of gunfire and the discharge of heavy tank guns.

The next morning the sun was bright and everything appeared normal. We went to the TV station where we were scheduled to record a week's worth of programming. Our series was played in three countries. "No wonder the enemy tried to stop us," Donna said. We were vulnerable but fortified by His angelic hosts. Nothing can thwart His purposes.

Now WOW – The Fluctuation Of Faith

Laughter fills the house. Three good days in succession ignites a joy and expectation, and the confidence that God has heard our prayers. For the first time in two months, she is able to lift herself from her chair and walk over to the piano in the next room. Praise and worship filled the house. Every indication is that things are getting back to normal. Bless the Lord! Because she was strong enough, we went for a short drive in the countryside. What a blessing! *A merry heart doeth good like a medicine: but a broken spirit drieth the bones.* (Proverbs 17:22)

Our jubilation however, was short lived. Late that afternoon, her condition took a dramatic turn for the worst. Her slide downward continues to accelerate. As I watch her weakening condition, I begin to question the dynamics of faith. Is my hope based on God's Word or is my faith built on the varying vicissitudes of circumstance? Hope that is based on evidence will vary with every changing situation. He who pins his faith to the stock market, a toilet seat or a pump-handle, will suffer many ups and downs. Alternatively, a hope that is based on the unshakable truths of God's Word shall never be shaken, regardless of the circumstances. This is certainly the import of Hebrews chapter eleven. Abel, Enoch, Noah, Abraham, Jacob and Sarah walked by faith, and all died without seeing their hope fulfilled. *These all died in faith, not having received the promises, but having seen them afar off, and were persuaded of them, and embraced them, and confessed that they were strangers and pilgrims on the earth.* (Hebrews 11:13)

The same account records the mighty exploits of faith accomplished by Moses, Joshua, Rahab, Gideon, Barak, Samson, Jephthae, David, Samuel, and the prophets. Their feats are awe inspiring and faith building indeed. However, the Bible also records mightier acts of faith preformed by unheralded nonentities, who are known only to God. These...*were tortured, not accepting deliverance... others had trial of cruel mockings and scourgings, yea, moreover of bonds and imprisonment: They were stoned, they were sawn asunder, were tempted, were slain with the sword: they wandered about in sheepskins and goatskins; being destitute, afflicted, tormented; (Of whom the world was not worthy:) they wandered in deserts, and in mountains, and in dens and caves of the earth.* <u>And these all, having obtained a good report through faith, received not the promise</u>... (Hebrew 11:37-40)

The goal of our faith must be brought into question. What is the objective of our faith? If the purpose is to achieve some personal goal or gain some advantage, or accumulate some commodity, then that faith is misguided. This is accomplished through conviction and self-motivation. You can do it. You have the ability. Don't be afraid. Go for it! If you succeed, there will be joy in the camp. If you fail, your hopes will be dashed until you pick up the pieces and start the process again. Never give up! God has ordained your good works. *For we are his workmanship, created in Christ Jesus unto good works, which God hath before ordained that we should walk in them.* (Ephesians 2:10) But this is not faith! It is personal confidence motivated by courage and hard work.

Faith is grounded in God and its sole purpose it to glorify Him! It is all about Him regardless of what happens to us. Job said, *Though he slay me, yet will I trust in him...*(Job 13:15) Queen Esther determined to...*go in unto the king, which is not according to the law: and* (said) *if I perish, I perish*. (Esther 4:16) Joseph, who was rejected, left for dead, sold into slavery and jailed, had faith in the purposes of God. *And Joseph said unto his brethren, Come near to me... And he said, I am Joseph your brother, whom ye sold into Egypt. Now therefore be not grieved, nor angry with yourselves, that ye sold me hither: for God did send me before you to preserve life.* (Genesis 45:4-5) Faith brings significance to the meaningless events of life. I find my wife's illness incomprehensible. She has faithfully served God since she was five years of age. Why she should be set aside at the prime of her influence is beyond my understanding. But if it is all about God, then our personal loss and pain is secondary.

In every thing give thanks: for this is the will of God in Christ Jesus concerning you. (1 Thessalonians 5:18)

WOW These are WordsOfWisdom we can live by!
><)))*>

Personal Challenge And Prayer Of Commitment

Presumption is never to be confused with faith. Those whom God sends are they that are under His protection. It has been said that, "God's will is His bill!" "If it is His baby,

He will kiss it!" The object is to first determine what His will is and then act upon it regardless of the circumstances. *Lead me, O LORD, in thy righteousness because of mine enemies; make thy way straight before my face.* (Psalms 5:8)

"Dear Lord: Lead me as You led Abraham's servant to find Rebecca, a wife for Isaac. *And he said, Blessed be the LORD God of my master Abraham, who hath not left destitute my master of his mercy and his truth: I being in the way, the LORD led me...* (Genesis 24:27). I pray this in the precious name of Jesus– Amen!"

Chapter 19

FAMILY GET-TO-GATHERS &
THE DISAPPOINTMENT OF FAITH

LOVE STORY – Family Get-to-gathers

Donna's mother, who vowed that she would never acknowledge a child from this marriage, would have been so proud and happy. By now, her offspring had grown to four married grandchildren, ten great grandchildren, three great-great grandchildren and an ever-expanding plethora of progeny. What forfeited blessing God had in store for her.

Thanksgiving, Christmas, Easter, anniversaries and birthdays were always special events in the Kent clan. Christmas however, was extraordinary. Everyone's home is decorated. Strings of lights outline the outside parameters of the entire house. Colorful lights illuminate the barren trees. Figures of the Nativity Scene are placed on the front lawn or the rooftops. The extravagance of the decoration is dependent on the motivation of each person.

An evergreen Christmas tree is cut down in the mountain forest and brought inside the house. It is given a special place and decorated with colorful lights that blink intermittently. Glass globes, icicles, ribbons, silver tinsel and artificial snow give it a fairytale wonderland look. Presents are carefully placed under the tree, with hardly enough room to contain them. Gifts wrapped in a variety of colors and shapes eagerly await their opening. The staircase is wreathed in a garland of green. A nativity scene is displayed depicting Mary, Joseph, the infant Jesus with the Wise man and their stock and camels. Dickens Village having some 25 ceramic houses portrays the Christmas Story. Stockings are hung on the fireplace mantle in hopes that they will be mysteriously filled with wonderful things during Christmas Eve. Then everyone bunkers down for the night wherever they can find an open space. Any place will do, the floor, the couch, the chandelier, anywhere.

Outside a snow blizzard may be blowing, but the inside is most inviting. A cozy warm fire burns in the fireplace. The aroma of freshly baked bread and sweets emanate from the kitchen and a large pot of apple cider simmers on the stove. Christmas dinner with the traditional turkey and all the trimmings that go with sumptuous dining highlights the day. Donna and I have worked endless hours to make this a memorable experience for our family.

Laughter fills the air, as friends and family forget the cares of daily life in lieu of fellowship. It is a time for celebration. All this "Festivity Making" is labor intensive, but it etches memories that are never forgotten. This Christmas was special. All our children made an effort to be present. It included a host of 22 persons.

Donna and I sit back on the couch and smile as the drama unfolds. The look of pleasure and screams of glee that come from the grandchildren are a joy to any grandparent. "We did this," said Donna, with the proudest look on her face.

That evening we fell into bed exhausted. "Thank you dear, for making all this happen. It was wonderful," I said. "We did it together. It was worth all the effort. What a wonderful Christmas Celebration," she responded! Little did we realize at that time, that this was to be our last time to be home for Christmas.

Now WOW - The Disappointment Of Faith

All incentive has left me. I feel empty, bankrupt! Shall I then immortalize my utter hopelessness with words that will only engender despair in others? How can I reconcile my faith with fact, and then translate that into feeling? How does one accept the harshness of reality when it is so inconsistent with the blessedness of faith? How can any rational mind put a positive spin on so great a tragedy? Is God any less God when fact grinds my feelings into anguish? "Does Jesus care when my heart is grieved too heavy for song or mirth, and my sad heart aches till it nearly breaks, is it aught to Him? Does He care?"

He sat at the foot of the bed and impassively said, "Your cancer is very aggressive. It's a hard fact of reality, but based on my experience, you have two to four weeks left. The best we can do is to make you comfortable." The room was stunned into silence as he left. What is there to say that hasn't already been said in forty-five years of togetherness. Words become meaningless sounds, trite attempts to ease the wrenching pain. We pressed our tear drenched faces together and wept.

In His conversation with John, Jesus indicated that he would live a long life and then magnify God by his death. *This He spoke, signifying by what death he would glorify God.* (John 21:19) The Greek word glorify is *daxad'zo*, and it means to magnify or to give full honor. Death is the act of giving full honor to God! It is little wonder then that David said, *Precious in the sight of the LORD, is the death of His saints.* (Psalms 116:15) In no way does this imply that God enjoys seeing the death of His children. To the contrary, the entire Psalm is dedicated to celebrating life! What the

Psalmist is saying is that life deeply matters to Him and He carefully guards our change of address.

Life is God's idea. Before the earth was formed, He specifically planned our being. *According as he hath chosen us in him before the foundation of the world...*(Ephesians 1:4) He alone is the Creator and Giver of life and He alone can take it. *For You formed my inward parts; You covered me in my mother's womb...I am fearfully and wonderfully made...My frame was not hidden from You, when I was made in secret, and skillfully wrought...Your eyes saw my substance, being yet unformed. And in Your book they all were written, the days fashioned for me, when as yet there were none of them.* (Psalms 139:13-16)

But what about faith, that mighty faith that sees God's promises and scoffs at impossibilities? What about that faith which is the substance of things hoped for, the evidence of things not seen? Where is that "mustard seed" faith that moves mountains into the sea? I have no logical explanation neither do I have any answers. All I know is that my faith is rooted in Him. It is relational rather than rational. The agony suffered by Job illustrates value of relationship over logic. *For I know that my redeemer liveth ... And though after my skin worms destroy this body, yet in my flesh shall I see God:* (Job 19:25-26) Although I cannot explain why my petitions have not been granted, I shall maintain my trust that He is able to save from the arms of death and the deepest grave.

Faith must sustain life's piercing disappointments. If it can't, it will fail you when you most need it. Faith does not cease to function in the face of death! We are people most miserable if we have faith for life only. This was Paul's import when he wrote, *If in this life only we have hope in Christ, we are of all men most miserable.* (1 Corinthians 15:19) Does Jesus care? "Oh yes He cares! I know He cares! His heart is touched with my grief. Though the way be weary, the long nights dreary, I know my Savior cares!"

But I would not have you to be ignorant, brethren, concerning them which are asleep, that ye sorrow not, even as others which have no hope. For if we believe that Jesus died and rose again, even so them also which sleep in Jesus will God bring with him. (1 Thessalonians 4:13-14)

WOW These are WordsOfWisdom we can live by!
><)))*>

Personal Challenge And Prayer Of Commitment

Life is filled with uncertainties. Trouble is inescapable. Disappointment is unavoidable. The intensity of pain that one suffers is directly proportionate to one's attitude and trust in God. It will hurt only as much as you allow it to hurt. *These things I have spoken unto you, that in me ye might have peace. In the world ye shall have tribulation: but be of good cheer; I have overcome the world.* (John 16:33)

"Dear Lord: I hurt. Help me to keep my mind focused on You and not on my present circumstances. I make a quality choice to comply with the admonition found in Isaiah. *Thou wilt keep him in perfect peace, whose mind is stayed on thee: because he trusteth in thee. Trust ye in the LORD for ever: for in the LORD JEHOVAH is everlasting strength*: (Isaiah 26:3-4) I pray this in the precious name of Jesus—Amen!"

Chapter 20

ONE ADVENTURE WE DIDN'T COUNT ON & THE ENDURANCE OF FAITH

LOVE STORY – One Adventure We Didn't Count On

Forty-four years of togetherness and going strong. Retirement was never an option for us. We were healthy, strong and motivated, furthermore, we were having too much fun. Life was truly a delight. We looked forward to the adventures of the next day; whatever that might bring us.

We had just completed a two-week tour of meetings. The first week we spent with friends at a business seminar. It was a time of fellowship and rest as well as ministry. The second week was spent at a large Marriage Advance held at a mountain lakeside camp-facility. Our relationship with the people of the Advance was more then ministry. We developed quality friendships and were repeat seminar speakers. As we came to the end of our last meeting, Donna challenged the audience with these words, "You have been so kind to us and we love you dearly. I don't know if we will ever be back again. Just know that God makes no mistakes. You can trust Him implicitly!" Her words were prophetic.

Donna's energy level appeared to be waning and she would rest a lot. Because of the heavy work schedule that we always carried, it was logical to assume that she was tired. Apart from one or two bruises that would come and go, she displayed no symptoms of any illness. So we continued to gallop together. We returned home to do a weekend ministry at our home church and spoke on the topic of entitled <u>The Need For Forgiveness</u>. We had four days together before I departed for a three-week tour of meetings. Donna stayed at home to rest. She would do some counseling, be with our children and maintain the home.

I arrived at the hotel and unpacked. Ten hours later, the telephone rang. It was my Donna. "Wilf," she said, "The doctor's biopsy report came in. I'm afraid the news is not good. I have Leukemia and been given 30 to 60 days to live." There was a numbing silence on both ends of the phone-line. How does one share such devastating news with someone so close as I was to her? As difficult as it was for me to receive it, it was more difficult for her to share. I was her flesh and blood, one person of two. How do I respond? She was my life!

There are no means to analyze feelings in such a crisis. We did what we had to do. I phoned my host and asked him to cancel all my meetings and to return me to the airport immediately. An entire eternity passed in the next few hours. Our minds raced back and forth over the past decades trying to find meaning and purpose to what was happening. There was none!

Her eight-hour wait for my return was unbearable. I was her safe place, but her safety was far removed. In a matter of hours the landing gear screeched on the landing strip. Two hours later we were admitted to the hospital for chemotherapy. A few lyrics of an old hymn ran continually through our minds. "All the way our Savior leads us, what have I to ask beside. Can I doubt His tender mercy, who through life has been our guide?"

The next four months were to be the most painful, yet

intimate and wonderful of our lives. She that served so many so faithfully all her life, was now totally dependant upon others. And others came willingly and eagerly to our rescue. My entire focus of concern was her welfare. Together we remembered, laughed and cried, hoped and prayed. Mostly we hoped and prayed. This is one adventure we hadn't counted on!

Now WOW - The Endurance Of Faith

My first job was selling cemetery lots when we were first married. As sales representatives we were not allowed to call them plots, lots or grave cites. Our pep-meetings instructed us how to convince people to "invest in cemetery properties". One central "pitch" went like this: "You don't want to go out on the worst day of your life, on a cold, wet or snowy day to buy a place to bury your loved one! Would you?" Indeed, it is prudent to be prepared for such a sad event. However, on the worst day of my life, forty-four years later, I went plodding through the snow to buy a grave cite for my loved one. What cruel irony and wrenching pain!

The day that I dreaded the most and sought so earnestly to avoid arrived with unrelenting force! Ending four and a half decades of blissful union cannot be easily accepted. She was my colleague and best friend. We worked together as a team at home, business and ministry. We saw each other as equals and gave careful deference to one another. I was a servant to her, and she to me. We had pleasure in filling these roles. Each choice we made was in the other person's favor. Our relationship was built upon respect and honor. Love is given without compensation, but respect and honor are earned. She had earned the esteem given her and she became a mother figure to many in the Body of Christ. The course materials that we taught from the platform, we lived in private. The principles on relationships that we have taught for years were more than academic rhetoric to us. My loss is incalculable!

My three daughters left their home and families and slept on the floor by her bedside for a week keeping watch. At three a.m. they came to my room and said, "Daddy, Mom is with Jesus!" For the first time in my life a paralyzing fear overpowered me. I had expected my grief to be so intense as to make me inconsolable. Instead, I knelt by her lifeless body, raised my hands heavenward, and brokenly sang, "All to Jesus, I surrender. All to Him I freely give. I will ever love and trust Him, in His presence daily live. I surrender all. I surrender all. All to Thee, my blessed Savior, I surrender all!" At that moment I gave Him my most precious possession, and with that came an overwhelming peace. A man is not wrong to release that which he cannot hold. In exchange he will gain a peace that he cannot earn.

But what about the faith you so fervently displayed? You claimed healing, but despite your fervor she died! How can one respond to such a question when every hope has been shattered into fragments? Because of my limited understanding I cannot see beyond the present or feel beyond the reach of my outstretched fingertips. I only know what is now, and right now know that I hurt. I also know that I must not and shall not succumb to my suffering, and so by faith I shall continue on continuing in faith.

By faith I must accept the promise that, *No temptation has seized* (me) *you except what is common to man. And God is faithful; he will not let* (me) *you be tempted beyond what* (I) *you can bear. But when* (I am) *you are tempted, he will also <u>provide a way out</u> so that* (I) *you can stand up under it.* (1 Corinthians 10:13) The word tempted (*pi'-rah*) does not refer to a drawing away into evil, but rather a trial or trouble.

My faith also gives me brief insights into what is in store for both my glorified partner and me. For her, she is welcomed into Glory with these words ... *Well done, thou good and faithful servant: thou hast been faithful over a few things, I will make thee ruler over many things: enter thou into the joy of thy Lord.* (Matthew 25:21, 23) For me, I am encouraged to continue the battle ... *be ye stedfast, unmoveable, always abounding in the work of the Lord, forasmuch as ye know that your labour is not in vain in the Lord.* (1 Corinthians 15:58)

Who shall separate us from the love of Christ? shall tribulation, or distress, or persecution, or famine, or nakedness, or peril, or sword ... in all these things we are more than conquerors through him that loved us. For I am persuaded, that neither death, nor life, nor angels, nor principalities, nor powers, nor things present, nor things to come, Nor height, nor depth, nor any other creature, shall be able to separate us from the love of God, which is in Christ Jesus our Lord. (Romans 8:35-39)

WOW These are WordsOfWisdom we can live by! ><)))*>

Personal Challenge And Prayer Of Commitment

All the way our Savior leads us. Indeed He does. Some through the valley, some through the flood, some through great sorrow but all through the blood. Never, never, never doubt His tender mercies. You can trust Him unconditionally.

"Dear Lord: Forgive me for my fear and doubt. Help me to endure hardness for the testimony of Christ. May I never bring shame to the cross by my attitude or behavior. I submit to Your will. This I pray this in the precious name of Jesus– Amen!"

Chapter 21

A KING WITH HIS CONSORT & THE PERSISTENCE OF FAITH

LOVE STORY – A King With His Consort

Donna had always been a woman of marked distinction. Statuesque in physical attributes, she displayed all the characteristics of maturity and dignified beauty. Even in her short and ravaging illness, she never lost her graces. To me, she was a goddess. How blessed I am to have had her as my wife.

I sat by her bedside daily. Long into the night I stayed with her until her breathing became heavy and I knew that she would sleep through the night. Then I would drive the long way home for a short sleep. To give me a break, our daughters, who had taken temporary leave from work, came to stay with their mom. How solicitous they were of their parents.

One day the Oncologist came in and stood by the bedside. "I would recommend that you contact Hospice," he said. "That is for terminally ill patients," Donna responded. "That is right. You are not going to get better. You are going to die. You may have a week left. The best we can do is to make you comfortable," he continued. "That's fine. I don't have to eat anymore," she said, and with that, she closed her eyes and fell into a peaceful sleep. In four short months, I saw a woman of strength waste away into a shell. Her appetite had left her long ago and she forced herself to eat in order to maintain her weight. All to no avail!

I went home and detailed the car. A fresh scent of pine filled the coach. I then took a shower, put on my best suit and tie and returned to the hospital to take my bride to her home. We had traveled thousands of miles together and the car became our sanctuary, a safe haven that we shared together. We discharged her from the hospital and wheeled her to the car for our trip home. She didn't see my suit or smell the fragrance of the pine freshener. She never spoke a word, but I felt as proud as a king with his consort. This was to be our last trip together.

Her comfort was our primary concern and so we set up a bed in front of the fireplace, with a view from a large window. Outside a winter's storm whirled snow in all directions. It was warm and cozy, full of life and activity inside, but she was unable to enjoy any of this. Her body was shutting down and she was too weak to move. I would come from behind the bed, lean over and bury my face in her pillow next to her head. To tell me that she knew I was there, she would press her cheek against mine. I would sing in her ear the many hymns and choruses we sang together as we traveled. When in Africa we learned of the Blackcollared Barbet, a brightly colored bird that warbled a beautiful song. The unusual thing was that when one sang, the mate would join in. We spent hours listening to their duet and considered ourselves to be their human counterpart. Although she had no strength to whisper, I knew that she was in duet with me, singing in perfect harmony.

"Sweetheart," I whispered. "Don't fight to stay on any longer. Don't worry about the children or me. We will be fine. I willingly release you. Jesus has come for you." I remained with my face next to hers for the longest time. Warm tears streamed down my face as I absorbed my last precious moments with her. Then I kissed her and went to bed.

She waited until three in the morning as if to make sure that everyone was in deep sleep so as not to disturb anyone. Then she left her body, took one last look around the home that was her palace and entered into the joy of the Lord. No more pain. No more suffering. No more sorrow. No more Earthly cares. Hers is the sweet reality of what she had been teaching for six decades. Her faith had become her reality. She has joined the Heavenly choir to sing in perfect harmony with the Redeemed Saints. And I too, continue to sing until the day that the Lord calls me to join them.

Now WOW - The Persistence Of Faith

Funerals are morbid events. They are characterized by agonizing pain, tears and grieving memories. Only a sadist can find macabre pleasure in death. People avoid funerals at all costs. But this was strikingly different. Her funeral service was magnificent! It evoked comments like "Splendid, Wonderful, Outstanding" and "Beautiful". But how can something so heartbreaking be beautiful?

People from all walks of life filled the 400-seat auditorium. The music was dignified and worshipful. The pastor gave her eulogy. The scripture and prayer offered by a friend. Her twenty children and grandchildren stood around the casket and presented their tribute, and a longtime family friend gave a message of comfort and hope. There was humor, honor, praise and tears, but the overriding sentiment was that of peace and an acceptance of His will. Memorial services were also held in Canada and South Africa.

By contrast, Graduation Exercises are always rewarding events. As educators, Donna and I attended many graduations events. Graduates would walk down the isle to an orchestral arrangement of <u>Pomp And Circumstance</u> and receive their hard earned degrees. They looked so smart dressed in their gowns and caps. An expression of self-esteem was reflected on each face, and rightly so. Donna greeted each graduate and congratulated them. Then I handed them their well-earned awards. Their years of study behind them, they now commenced a new life.

This was no funeral for Donna. It was her Graduation and Commencement Service. After her accolades were presented, the congregation stood at attention and she was carried to her waiting coach to the music of <u>Pomp And Circumstance</u>.

As beautiful as was the ceremony, it was soon overshadowed by a numbing silence and solitude. I could see the vacant stare in my children's faces as they struggled to control their emotions. Some didn't. Overwhelmed by my own grief I found it difficult to offer any consolation. All I could think is why? Why God? The Lord spared our lives from sure-death experiences on several occasions. We knew without doubt that His everlasting arms were around us. There was no question that angels, God's ministering spirits, were dispatched to protect us. It was this knowledge that enabled us to serve Him for twenty years in foreign countries without any pledge of financial support or health insurance. In all that time we were never without and never sick. We had witnessed His healing powers in others and were convinced to the end, that He would do the same for us, again. Then why would He choose to ignore the volume of prayer that assaulted His Throne on our behalf? Why would He permit this untimely death now? I don't know.

The word untimely is a concept that applies only to here and now. Eternity is never late. It is always timely. Solomon declared that God *makes all things beautiful in His time!* (Ecclesiastes 3:11) It is evident that my timeline differs radically from God's schedule. And so reluctantly but willingly, I surrender my agenda to Him and with that, my beloved

Donna. With Paul the Apostle, she can declare her testimony, *I have fought a good fight, I have finished my course, I have kept the faith: Henceforth there is laid up for me a crown of righteousness, which the Lord, the righteous judge, shall give me at that day: and not to me only, but unto all them also that love his appearing.* (2 Timothy 4:7-8) My Precious Darling graduated and with that, she exchanged her graduation cap for a crown. What a graduation!

The house is full of her handiwork. Her creative fingerprints are seen on everything she touched. Each a reminder of what used to be. Emotions of sorrow are frequent, but to wallow in the quagmire of self-pity is neither pleasing to God nor productive to man. And so I look forward to tomorrow, and tomorrow and tomorrow, sorrowing but not as those who have no hope. God has a plan for each life and by His Grace we are determined to fulfill it!

Therefore, my beloved brethren, be ye stedfast, unmoveable, always abounding in the work of the Lord, forasmuch as ye know that your labour is not in vain in the Lord. (1 Corinthians 15:58)

WOW These are **W**ords**O**f**W**isdom we can live by!
><)))*>

Personal Challenge And Prayer Of Commitment

You are never alone, when you are alone. Nor will you be abandoned to your own recourse. He is your solace and consolation. In your deepest need He will be your safeguard. *For we do not have a high priest who is unable to sympathize with our weaknesses, but we have one who has been tempted in every way, just as we are—yet was without sin. Let us then approach the throne of grace with confidence, so that we may receive mercy and find grace to help us in our time of need.* (Hebrews 4:15-16)

"Dear Lord: You understand my pain. I lean on You heavily. I have no strength or direction but that which You provide. *Therefore with joy shall ye draw water out of the wells of salvation. And in that day shall ye say, Praise the LORD* ...(Isaiah 12:3-4) Today Lord, I drink deeply from Your well. I pray this in the precious name of Jesus – Amen!"

Chapter 22

A Peek Into Heaven & The Cry Of Faith

Love Story – A Peek Into Heaven

To ease my pain, I have asked the Lord to give me a glimpse into Heaven. "Lord, give me a vision, a dream, just one small peek to see her dancing before You!" As yet, I am still waiting. Nothing beyond the ordinary mundane routine has overpowered me! But what I can see by faith dissipates my clouds of doubt, and I can see clearly now.

From my understanding of scripture, Paul knew a man that ... *was caught up to paradise. He heard inexpressible things, things that man is not permitted to tell.* (2 Corinthians 12:4) Commentators believe that he was speaking of his own experiences when he was beaten and stoned. Later he gives this testimony, *I am torn between the two: I desire to depart and be with Christ, which is better by far; but it is more necessary for you that I remain in the body.* (Philippians 1:23-24)

Perhaps this is the only glimpse I shall have of heaven, this side of my own death. His Word is sufficient to engender faith, generate hope and provoke courage for the future, but I miss her. I know that all is well, but I still miss her. As wonderful as our fairytale marriage was, I would never recall her from what she is experiencing back to this life. But I miss her. I fill my day with Earthly routine in a futile attempt to dampen my Heavenly preoccupations, but I miss her. Our children, now far beyond their insufferable teen-years are an amazing comfort to me, but I miss her.

My children and grandchildren also need comfort. Not blessed with the years that have granted me wisdom and experience, they depend on Daddy for support. I seek to console by telling them that the mind has a remarkable filtering mechanism called a "forgetter". With the passage of time, the pain and distasteful images will pass giving way to pleasant memories and meaning.

Despite our quiet yearning for "Mom" we take refuge in the glimpse of Heaven provided in His Word. And God shall wipe away all tears from their eyes; and there shall be no more death, neither sorrow, nor crying, neither shall there be any more pain: for the former things are passed away. (Revelation 21:4)

Blessed be the God and Father of our Lord Jesus Christ, which according to his abundant mercy hath begotten us again unto a lively hope by the resurrection of Jesus Christ from the dead, To an inheritance incorruptible, and undefiled, and that fadeth not away, reserved in heaven for you, Who are kept by the power of God through faith unto salvation ready to be revealed in the last time. Wherein ye greatly rejoice, though now for a season, if need be, ye are in heaviness through manifold temptations: That the trial of your faith, being much more precious than of gold that perisheth, though it be tried with fire, might be found unto praise and honour and glory at the appearing of Jesus Christ: Whom having not seen, ye love; in whom, though now ye see him not, yet believing, ye rejoice with joy unspeakable and full of glory: Receiving the end of your faith, even the salvation of your souls. (1 Peter 1:3-9)

Strange! For some inexplicable reason, it is as though

she has never been here, or she has never left or she is always present. Without some misguided attempt to deify her, she has become synonymous with Jesus. As part of the Bride of Christ, she has joined the countless saints to become "one flesh" with Him. Is this what Peter was saying when he penned the following words? *But now in Christ Jesus you who once were far away have been brought near through the blood of Christ. For he himself is our peace, who has made the two one and has destroyed the barrier, the dividing wall of hostility, by abolishing in his flesh the law with its commandments and regulations. <u>His purpose was to create in himself one new man out of the two</u>, thus making peace, and in this one body to reconcile both of them to God through the cross, by which he put to death their hostility. He came and preached peace to you who were far away and peace to those who were near. For through him we both have access to the Father by one Spirit.* (Ephesians 2:13-18)

With countless others, I too look for that city ... *which hath foundations, whose builder and maker is God.* (Hebrews 11:10)

Now WOW - The Cry Of Faith

When no one is around, I cry. I tell myself that she is in a far better place and I would not bring her back, but I cry. My faith is anchored in the fact that God makes no mistakes, but I still cry. The condolences of many friends comfort me, but I cry. Despite the hurt, a peace fills the house and a sense of His divine presence succors me. I am energized with a confidence for the future, but I cry. Is that incongruous? Is it wrong for a gown man to cry? Does it display a lack of faith? Is it wrong to miss the one you have loved so dearly, and who has been your companion for more than four decades? I think not!

Abraham grieved for his wife. *And Sarah died ... and*

Abraham came to mourn for Sarah, and to weep for her. (Genesis 23:2) All of Israel grieved for Aaron. *And when all the congregation saw that Aaron was dead, they mourned for Aaron thirty days, even all the house of Israel.* (Numbers 20:29) King David cried when he penned *...put thou my tears into thy bottle: are they not in thy book?* (Psalms 56:8) At the grave of Lazarus, *Jesus wept.* (John 11:35)

The difference between self-pity and genuine mourning is striking. The first is a preoccupation with one's self and painful emotions. These are tormenting, debilitating and can develop into chronic depression and long-term anxiety. They exert harmful influences on relationships and negatively affect productivity. Furthermore, it is sinful! It is an affront to God who has promised *...I will be with you; I will never leave you nor forsake you.* (Joshua 1:5) It is disobedience to God's command *...The Lord is near. Do not be anxious about anything...* (Philippians 4:5-6) Jesus challenged His disciples: *"Therefore I tell you, do not worry about your life...* (Luke 12:22) Self-indulging nostalgia looks longingly over the shoulder to a fading memory of yesterday, a Camelot that once may have existed but is no more. Conversely, grieving is the mourning for the loss. It is not egocentric. Mourning is centered more on the loss than on the person experiencing the loss. Abraham mourned <u>for</u> Sarah. The congregation mourned <u>for</u> Aaron. The object of the weeping was for the individual.

We prayed for her healing for months. Our faith was energized by many Scriptural promises. Countless people from all parts of the world held prayer vigils on her behalf. Many churches placed her on their prayer-chains. More than one thousand E-mails from all quarters of the globe were received, encouraging us with their faith and prayer. We had faith that God would heal her. If her healing was contingent on faith alone, then she would be doing handsprings down the streets and cartwheels in the intersection! However, another dynamic was also at work; His Sovereign will. God alone is the giver of life and He chose to take her. Clearly, this is underscored in our Lord's prayer, *My Father, if it is possible, may this cup be taken from me. Yet not as I will, but as you will.* (Matthew 26:39)

In the turmoil of my mind and emotions, I rejoice with her and cry for her at the same time. When I find myself slipping from grieving into a self-pity mode, I counsel myself with meaningless clichés like, "Wilf, this is your garden. Dig it", "Wilf, this too shall come to pass" and "Wilf, shape up". It helps a little. However, my real comfort comes from my grieving, and my strength form the Lord. King David found this to be true when his child died. *David pleaded with God for the child. He fasted and went into his house and spent the nights lying on the ground... and he would not eat any food... On the seventh day the child died... Then David got up from the ground. After he had washed, put on lotions and changed his clothes, he went into the house of the LORD and worshiped...* [Then he said] *now that he is dead, why should I fast? Can I bring him back again? I will go to him, but he will not return to me."* (2 Samuel 12:16-23)

The sun was not up when I awakened this morning. As I was getting dressed I found myself singing. *"Great is Thy faithfulness, Oh God my Father. There is no shadow in turning with thee. Thou changest not, Thy compassions, they fail not; As Thou hast been, Thou forever will be. Great is thy faithfulness. Great is Thy faithfulness. Morning by morning new mercies I see. All I have need thy hand hath provided – Great is thy faithfulness, Lord unto me!* Thank you Lord. It has been a good day.

...weeping may remain for a night, but rejoicing comes in the morning. (Psalms 30:5)

WOW These are WordsOfWisdom we can live by!
><)))*>

Personal Challenge And Prayer Of Commitment

There is no better challenge than is found in the words of an old hymn.

> "Are you weary, are you heavy-hearted?
>   Tell it to Jesus, tell it to Jesus.
> Are you grieving over joys departed?
>   Tell it to Jesus alone.
> Do you fear the gath'ring clouds of sorrow?
>   Tell it to Jesus, tell it to Jesus.
> Are you anxious what shall be tomorrow?
>   Tell it to Jesus alone.
> Tell it to Jesus, tell it to Jesus.
>   He is a friend that's well known.
> You have no other such a friend or brother.
>   Tell it to Jesus alone."

If in this life only we have hope in Christ, we are of all men most miserable. But now is Christ risen from the dead, and become the firstfruits of them that slept. (1 Corinthians 15:19-20)

"Dear Lord: You have given me hope, not only for today but for life hereafter. By Your strength I make a quality choice to live in victory. You have created me "unto good works" and by Your help I am determined to achieve them. I pray this in the precious name of Jesus – Amen!"

Chapter 23

EARS TO HEAR & THE GLORIES OF FAITH

LOVE STORY – Ears To Hear

The afternoon shadows lengthen as they reach out to meet the darkness. I sit alone in my large, well-appointed four-bedroom home. All is quiet except for the mating calls of the crickets. As I contemplate my life I begin to realize how little I have in common with this world. The evening news is blatant political propaganda, comedy sitcoms underscore hidden agendas, special interest groups promote their philosophies, newspapers are filled with advertising, and countless other clarion voices call for my attention promoting their meaningless tripe. Cynical? Perhaps. But it is more accurate than not. So I shut everything off and read my Bible. I am beginning to understand what the early Saints meant when they ... *confessed that they were strangers and pilgrims on the earth.* (Hebrews 11:13) Peter also underscores the same sentiment when he challenges ... *Dearly beloved, I beseech you as strangers and pilgrims, abstain from fleshly lusts, which war against the soul* (1 Peter 2:11)

By no means am I lonely or disconsolate. Just today I joined the disciples and walked the Shores of Galilee, as

Jesus taught the parable of the sower and the seed. He is a very impressive teacher, you know. After the parable He charged, "He that has ears to hear, let him hear". "Now why does He say that," I wonder? Everyone I know has ears. I know that not everyone that has ears hears or understands. But is there more to his charge than is the obvious? Indeed there is. Jesus finishes the sentence He begins in the Gospels, at the end of the Bible. In the book of Revelation chapters 2 and 3, He challenges the seven churches of Asia with these words. "He that hath ears to hear, let him hear what the Spirit says to the churches." ... *hear what the Spirit says....*

I have read this portion countless times and understand the theology. But today I realize that I have been insensitive to the voice of the Spirit. Then a "flash-back" occurred as I remembered a Squatter Camp in South Africa where Donna and I have frequently ministered. There are no streets, lights, running water or sewage systems. A million people live here in cardboard shacks and tin huts. With 75 percent unemployment, many people have little to eat. These poverty stricken souls have little of this worlds goods, but we have seen a thousand people rich in the spirit, standing with their hands upraised in praise to God singing, "Holy Spirit, move me now. Make my life whole again..." Quietly I begin to hum the melody that has become so familiar. Then in a faint whisper I mouth the words and then with tears streaming down my face and uplifted arms I brake into full song, "Holy Spirit, move me now. Make my life whole again..." This is the *walk in the Spirit that* (Galatians 5:16,25) that gives meaning to life.

God communicates with mankind through the agency of His Spirit. This is the import of Romans 8:16. *The Spirit Himself bears witness with our spirit...* Fish communicate with fish, birds with birds and man with mankind. And the Spirit of God communicates with the spirit of man. God's Spirit cannot communicate with the intellect of man anymore than a bird can transmit information to a fish. However, God's Spirit can and does communicate with His Spirit that He has placed within man. The Apostle James makes this clear when he tells us that God's Spirit yearns our fellowship and is jealous for our attentiveness. *Or do you think Scripture says without reason that the spirit he caused to live in us <u>envies</u>* [epipotheow - to yearn, desire, greatly long for] *intensely?* (James 4:5) In simple terms, God jealously desires to fellowship with the us through His Spirit that He placed within us.

I am inclined to mistake my own common sense reasoning for the witness of the Spirit. God's Spirit however, can witnesses only to the Spirit nature that is in us and not the brain that directs us. That is why Jesus said, "He that hath ears to hear, <u>let him hear what the Spirit says</u> to the churches."

"Lord, my intellect is overpowered by the events that You have allowed in my life. I don't understand them. But then, my understanding is futile in knowing Your purposes. I have studied Your word but have failed to hear Your Spirit. Holy Spirit, move me now. Communicate with my regenerated spirit the will of the Father. – Amen"

But as it is written, Eye hath not seen, nor ear heard, neither have entered into the heart of man, the things which God hath prepared for them that love him. But God hath revealed them unto us by his Spirit: for the Spirit searcheth all things, yea, the deep things of God. For what man knoweth the things of a man, save the spirit of man which is in him? even so the things of God knoweth no man, but the Spirit of God. Now we have received, not the spirit of the world, but the spirit which is of God; that we might know the things that are freely given to us of God. (1 Corinthians 2:9-12)

Now WOW - The Glories Of Faith

It is highly presumptuous for me to write about the wonder of death since I have never experienced it. It is a mystery that is revealed only upon death. Because we live in a society that requires incontrovertible scientific evidence, the subjective testimony of man is viewed with skepticism and suspicion. Yet the testimony of others cannot be easily discarded.

Paul the Apostle had an after death experience. He was so overwhelmed that he had no words to describe it, neither was he allowed to tell of the event. In relating his near death experience, he tells us ... *I knew a man in Christ above fourteen years ago, (whether in the body, I cannot tell; or whether out of the body, I cannot tell: God knoweth;) such an one caught up to the third heaven. And I knew such a man, ...How that he was caught up into paradise, and heard unspeakable words, which it is not lawful for a man to utter.* (2 Corinthians 12:2-4)

Stephan became the first Christian to be martyred for his faith. As he was being stoned, the Glory of heaven was manifested to him. *...they gnashed on him with their teeth. But he, being full of the Holy Ghost, looked up stedfastly into heaven, and saw the glory of God, and Jesus standing on the right hand of God, And said, Behold, I see the heavens opened, and the Son of man standing on the right hand of God ... And they stoned Stephen, calling upon God, and saying, Lord Jesus, receive my spirit... And when he had said this, he fell asleep.* (Acts 7:54-60) The preview that Stephan received of Heaven diminished the painful reality of his death into drab insignificance.

<u>The Bloody Theater</u> also known as <u>Martyrs Mirrors</u>, complied by Thieleman J. Van Braght, is a 1157 page documentary of the unspeakable torture and slaughter of countless defenseless Christians, that willingly laid down their lives for the testimony of Christ. The book records the actual court proceedings (from the time of Christ to the year 1660) of the merciless interrogations of Christian believers and their responses. Significant is their gracious acceptance of

torture and executions. Despite their overwhelming loss, they refused to deny their faith in Jesus. In each instance ... *they overcame him by the blood of the Lamb, and by the word of their testimony; and they loved not their lives unto the death.* (Revelation 12:11) The book of Hebrews testifies of such faithful when it states that ... *others were tortured, not accepting deliverance; that they might obtain a better resurrection* (Hebrews 11:35)

Jesus told John that he would live a lengthy life and then die from old age. *This spake he, signifying by what death he should glorify God...*(John 21:19) John's death is described as a means by which he glorified God! Perhaps death is given more recognition that it deserves. Rather than fearing death, maybe it should be greeted?

As a young seminary graduate I recall pastoring one of my churches. An elder of the congregation was in the hospital on oxygen and intravenous awaiting his release; but not from the hospital. I came to encourage him in his struggle for survival. What I found was a man with a smile that rose above his pain and an eager anticipation of his release. "It can't be long now Pastor. Can it," he would ask? He was totally removed from the concerns of life. His home, the garden and the mass of stuff he had accumulated, now meant nothing to him. "It can't be long now, Pastor. Can it?" Forty long years have passed since that incident but the image is fixed clearly in my mind, and the lessons I learned from this dying man have served to engender my life to faithfulness. "It can't be long now Pastor. Can it?"

I love life! Everyday is an adventure. Opportunities abound with each passing moment and I don't want to miss any of them. I pray for longevity and significance. But I too, yearn for the glories of my release and long to be joined to my Lord and loved ones.

Therefore, my beloved brethren, be ye stedfast, unmoveable, always abounding in the work of the Lord, forasmuch as ye know that your labour is not in vain in the Lord. (1 Corinthians 15:58)

WOW   These are WordsOfWisdom we can live by!
><)))*>

Personal Challenge And Prayer Of Commitment

If you have never heard the voice of God's Spirit, it may be that your spirit has never been made alive. Only Jesus can make a dead thing live. Ask Jesus who is the Resurrection and the Life to come and live within you. Even as He raise Lazarus from the dead, He will make your Spirit alive. It may also be that although God's Spirit dwells in you, your mind is so preoccupied with the cares of life that you cannot hear Him. "He that hath ears to hear, let him hear what the Spirit says to the churches." ... *hear what the Spirit says....*

"Dear Lord: I am sorry for being so preoccupied with my concerns that I have not heard You. Forgive me for grieving You with my insensitivity. Holy Spirit, move me now. Make my life whole again! I pray this in the precious name of Jesus – Amen!"

Chapter 24

IT IS WELL WITH MY SOUL & THE PRODUCT OF FAITH

LOVE STORY – It Is Well With My Soul

The lyrics and story of an old hymn that made an impression on me during my early Christian walk comes clearly back into my memory. Millions of grief-stricken people have taken comfort from the author's tragedy. Today, he has been a solace to me.

Horatio G. Spafford (1825-1888) was a wealthy real estate developer in Chicago. He was a devout Christian and supporter of Dwight L. Moody. His wife Anna, four daughters and son lived in an upscale part of the city. Despite his upright life, he was tested severely. His young son died from an epidemic. The Chicago burn in 1871 wiped out the city as well as his entire empire. He purchased six tickets to go to England but before they were able to board the ship, he was called back to Chicago for business. He put his wife and four daughters aboard with the promise that he would join them soon. Later that month he received a cryptic telegram from his wife Anna. It read, "Saved alone". Half way across the ocean, the ship collided with another resulting in an enormous loss of life.

Their four daughters drowned. Several months later, he boarded a ship that was to bring his reunion with his beloved family. When the ship reached the spot where the tragedy occurred, the Captain announced that it was near this spot that the ship sank. He would have found his grief inconsolable were it not for his faith in God's Sovereign will. Looking at the waters below through tears that obscured his vision, he penned the following words:

> "When peace like a river attendeth my way,
> when sorrows like sea-billows roll,
>   What ever my lot, Thou hast taught me to say,
> "It is well, it is well with my soul.
>   Though Satan should buffet, tho' trials should come,
> let this blest assurance control,
>   That Christ hath regarded my helpless estate,
> And hath shed His own blood for my soul.
>   My sin - oh, the bliss of this glorious thought –
> My sin, not in part but the whole,
>   Is nailed to the cross, and I bear it no more;
> Praise the Lord, praise the Lord, O my soul.
>   And Lord haste the day when my faith shall be sight,
> The clouds be rolled back as a scroll,
>   The trump shall resound, and the Lord shall descend,
> 'Even so', it is well with my soul."

Death is never a pleasant prospect. It announces the end of everything that has gone on before. No one wants to terminate a good thing or a wonderful relationship. I may have lost the love of my life, but I haven't lost my trust in Him. For the child of God, there are two facts that engender peace and hope.

The first is that Jesus was tested in every way as we are. He fully understands our frame and is therefore able and eager to uphold those that are likewise tested. Paul clearly underscores this fact in Hebrews 4:14-16. *Therefore, since we have a great high priest who has gone through the heavens, Jesus the Son of God, let us hold firmly to the faith we profess. For we do not have a high priest who is unable to sympathize with our weaknesses, but we have one who has been tempted in every way, just as we are—yet was without sin. Let us then approach the throne of grace with confidence, so that we may receive mercy and find grace to help us in our time of need.*

The second thing that inspires hope is the fact that the end of one thing always signals the beginning of something new. For I know the thoughts that I think toward you, saith the LORD, thoughts of peace, and not of evil, to give you an expected end. Then shall ye call upon me, and ye shall go and pray unto me, and I will hearken unto you. And ye shall seek me, and find me, when ye shall search for me with all your heart. (Jeremiah 29:11-13)

It is said that there are five hymns that have changed the course of human history. <u>What A Friend We Have In Jesus</u>, <u>Amazing Grace</u>, <u>Silent Night</u>, <u>How Great Thou Art</u> and <u>It Is Well With My Soul</u>! In each instance, these hymns were penned from the anguish of great tragedy. As a child of God, I sorrow but not as one that has no hope. I can truly say it is well with my soul.

Now WOW - The Product Of Faith

Philosophically, I can say that I never have a bad day! Some days are much better that others, but each day is a good day. This day however, is not the better of my "good days." As a matter of fact, it ranks among the worst of my "good days." Biblically, *this is the day that the Lord hath made.* (Psalms 118:24) I should then *rejoice and be glad therein.* But herein lies the problem. My humanity has a difficult time keeping up with my philosophy and theology.

Memories flood my mind of yesteryear. Within a few moments after seeing her for the first time, I nudged my college roommate and said, "I'm going to marry that girl!" Little did I realize at the time how true that was to become. Splendidly Junoesque, I sat riveted to my seat watching her every move. She looked like a goddess to me. Memories! Our courtship, our wedding, our family times, our friends and the years of ministry became crystal clear as I roamed the quiet archive of my mind. Echoes of "what-it-used-to-be" resonate throughout my memories. I can quickly lose myself in reflective thought. One cannot easily set aside so rich a heritage. Neither do I intend to. Past experiences are vital to what we become. They form the very foundations upon which future structures are built. To crater now is to trash four decades of preparation!

A young couple named Lester and Jeannie, was called to North Africa as missionaries. They took their two small children and left for France to study the language. Before they were able to unpack and settle in, Lester was killed in a motorcycle accident. Three months after she returned with her children, she phoned and asked for an appointment to see us. We were fully prepared to do grief counseling. Surprisingly, this was not the case. Her story was heart wrenching. "The rumor is going around the church" she said, "that Les and I must have had a bad marriage because I am not an emotional basket-case. Some have suggested that I am glad he is dead, and others said that I must have another man on the scene. How can I tell them that the peace of God fills my heart and mind? How do I convey the overriding comfort and hope and confidence that He gives me? The children ask 'Mommy, when is daddy coming home?' I reach out to his side of the bed to touch him, but he's not there. Tears run down my face and my heart aches as though it could break. Despite my pain, His comfort is so real that each day is joy to me. How do I convey that?"

Years later, I discovered exactly what she was talking about. God's overwhelming peace so fills the house that sorrow flees and pain diminishes into drab insignificance. I almost feel guilty at feeling so complete. According to books written on death and dying and the stages of grieving, I should be writhing in turmoil over my loss. This may be true of those that have no hope. Evidently, the secular experts of grief management know little about the *peace of God that passes all human understanding.* (Philippians 4:4-9) Because they have never been correctly informed, the only conclusion they can reach is grief. How different for the child of God. *Brothers, we do not want you to be ignorant about those who fall asleep, or to grieve like the rest of men, who have no hope. We believe that Jesus died and rose again and so we believe that God will bring with Jesus those who have fallen asleep in him.* (1 Thessalonians 4:13-14)

God's has His purpose in everything. Jesus earnestly pleaded, *My Father, if it is possible, may this cup be taken from me.* (Matthew 26:39) He then continued ...*Yet not as I will, but as <u>you will</u>.* Despite my prayer for her recovery, He willed to take her home. "Lord, what do <u>You will</u> now?" The lessons learned from our mourning must not be lost to despondency. One reason for the trials we experience is found in Paul's admonition to the early Christians at Corinth.

Praise be to the God and Father of our Lord Jesus Christ, the Father of compassion and the God of all comfort, who comforts us in all our trouble, so that we can comfort those who are in any trouble with the comfort we ourselves have received from God. (2 Corinthians 1:3-4)

WOW! These are **W**ords**O**f**W**isdom we can live by >>)))*>

A Personal Challenge And Prayer Of Commitment

The death of Moses was a shock to the people. Joshua was his heir apparent and the challenge that God gave him must inspire every follower of God. *Now after the death of Moses the servant of the LORD it came to pass, that the LORD spake unto Joshua the son of Nun, Moses' minister, saying, Moses my servant is dead; now therefore arise, go over this Jordan, thou, and all this people, unto the land which I do give to them, even to the children of Israel. Every place that the sole of your foot shall tread upon, that have I given unto you, as I said unto Moses. From the wilderness and this Lebanon even unto the great river, the river Euphrates, all the land of the Hittites, and unto the great sea toward the going down of the sun, shall be your coast. There shall not any man be able to stand before thee all the days of thy life: as I was with Moses, so I will be with thee: I will not fail thee, nor forsake thee. Be strong and of a good courage: for unto this people shalt thou divide for an inheritance the land, which I sware unto their fathers to give them. Only be thou strong and very courageous, that thou mayest observe to do according to all the law, which Moses my servant commanded thee: turn not from it to the right hand or to the left, that thou mayest prosper whithersoever thou goest. This book of the law shall not depart out of thy mouth; but thou shalt meditate therein day and night, that thou mayest observe to do according to all that is written therein: for then thou shalt make thy way prosperous, and then thou shalt have good success. Have not I commanded thee? Be strong and of a good courage; be not afraid, neither be thou dismayed: for the LORD thy God is with thee whithersoever thou goest.* (Joshua 1:1-9)

"Dear Lord: Restore my life and make it anew. Have Your perfect way in me. Whatever it is that You wish to accomplish in and through me, do. I willingly submit to Your will. I pray this in the precious name of Jesus – Amen!"

Chapter 25

THE REFINING FIRES & THE WILDERNESS OF FAITH

LOVE STORY – The Refining Fires

One quickly recognizes the enormous help that the Body of Christ provides when tragedy strikes. It is easy to take the love and support of God's family for granted, until we find ourselves in a critical situation. My family and I have benefited greatly from the support we have received from the Christian community. Thank you for walking with us through our valley. To every child of God that has ever helped anyone, "Thank you for giving to the Lord!"

Donna and I had a model marriage. One would think that I would be totally devastated by my loss. Remarkably, that is not so. The house is not empty; I am not sad, I sleep soundly and awaken expecting to see what God has in store for today. That is not normal. It is supernatural! I do grieve and have my times of "self-pity." I guess that is natural. When that happens, God reminds me that He has promised to be a *"mate to the mate-less and a father to the fatherless."* (Psalms 68:4-5)

God specializes in making order out of chaos. As a matter of fact, chaos is the very process that He often uses to bring about order. The secularist defines the process of evolution as "thesis, antithesis and synthesis." Thesis is the order of things as we have made it. Along comes the confusion and disorder created by antithesis. When all the pieces fall apart and dissipate, they come together in synthesis as a new order. Then the process starts all over again. This is the very notion that drives Communism. When one deletes God from the equation, he is left with nothing but chaos. I prefer to see God's hand at work in the affairs of man.

The "Big Bang" that created the universe was not proceeded by the word "Oops". God used natural forces to bring about the magnificent order seen in the stellar heavens. The Tragedy brought about by Adam and Eve in the Garden of Eden was not a tragedy. God was bringing into being a new race of people called Christians by the obedience of Jesus, the Last Adam. (1 Corinthians 15:45-50) Israel's adulterous disobedience and their resulting wilderness wandering produced a people that acknowledged God as the Lover of their souls. And me? Is there any redeeming reason for my chaos? Indeed there is! Peter underscores this clearly. *Wherein ye greatly rejoice, though now for a season, if need be, ye are in heaviness through manifold temptations: That the trial of your faith, being much more precious than of gold that perisheth, though it be tried with fire, might be found unto praise and honour and glory at the appearing of Jesus Christ: Whom having not seen, ye love; in whom, though now ye see him not, yet believing, ye rejoice with joy unspeakable and full of glory: Receiving the end of your faith, even the salvation of your souls.* (1 Peter 1:6-9)

We had the privilege of seeing gold mined and refined. A Mine-Captain took us seven thousand, five hundred feet below ground to the very face of the rock where miners were working. The experience was frightening for sunshine lovers. Tons of granite are then crushed and molten to produce one ounce of gold. A heating process brings all the scum and debris to the surface where it is skimmed off and discarded. The more the heating process is repeated, the more scum is removed and the purer the gold becomes. We were told that gold in its purest form is transparent.

Unknown to me, there is a lot of rubbish that lays hidden in my life. As the fires grew hotter, I became amazed at the debris that kept bubbling to the surface. His goal is to purify me and make me into His likeness. So I thank the Lord that God has found me sufficiently faithful to try me in the furnace of adversity. My earnest prayer is that I will be found faithful and that through my pain, I may be able to bring solace to others.

King David prayed, *Take away the dross from the silver, and there shall come forth a vessel for the finer. Take away the wicked from before the king, and his throne shall be established in righteousness* (Proverbs 25:4-5) Job declared, *But he knoweth the way that I take: when he hath tried me, I shall come forth as gold.* (Job 23:10)

Now WOW - The Wilderness Of Faith

Since God makes no mistakes, my train wreck must be a work of art. Great! How something as traumatic as losing one's mate can be beautiful, is a mystery beyond comprehension. It gives new meaning to clichés like "Bitter sweet sorrow", or "Good grief" or "It was the worst of times, it was the best of times." My first impulse is to reject these as meaningless phrases. Each concept is an oxymoron at best. Yet, God often shows His grand design through adversity. This is the import of Peter's admonition; *Wherein ye greatly rejoice, though now for a season, if need be, ye are in heaviness through <u>manifold temptations</u>* [suffer grief of all kinds of trails]*: That the trial of your faith, being much more precious than of gold* [of greater worth than gold] *that perisheth, though it be tried with fire, might be found unto* *praise and honour and glory at the appearing of Jesus Christ.* (1 Peter 1:6-7) The lyrics of the old hymn, <u>Let The Beauty Of Jesus Be Seen In Me</u> may display sincerity, but if we knew the paths that God would lead us through to achieve this purpose, we would sing it less enthusiastically.

Do I enjoy my loss? No. Only a masochist finds pleasure in pain. Must I put on my "happy face" to cover my hurt? No. That would be denial. Must I pretend that my devotion is so strong that I can treat my sorrow with indifference? No. That is what psychologists call reaction formation. Do I confess it away? No. Then I must acknowledge defeat? No! Must I wallow in the mire of self-absorbing despondency? No! Do I marinade in the juices of my own self-pity? No! Then what must I do? The answer is as simple as it is revolutionary. Recognize that God is working out His divine plan in your life. There is a grand design to your chaos. The final result will diminish the glory of the former into drab insignificance.

Such was the case of the children of Israel. The story of their wilderness experience is found in Hosea 2:14-16. *Therefore, behold, <u>I will allure her</u>* [God's...Motivation], *and <u>bring her into the wilderness</u>* [Isolation], *and <u>speak comfortably unto her</u>* [Consolation]. *And I will <u>give her vineyards</u> from thence* [Provision], *and the valley of <u>Achor</u>* (meaning trouble) *for <u>a door of hope</u>* [Anticipation]: *and <u>she shall sing there</u>* [Jubilation], *<u>as in the days of her youth</u>* [Restoration], *and as in the day when she <u>came up out of</u> the land of Egypt* [Liberation]. *And it shall be <u>at that day saith the LORD</u>* [Intention], *that thou shalt <u>call me Ishi</u>* (meaning husband); *and <u>shalt call me no more Baali</u>* (meaning master) [Completion].

A wilderness is a foreboding place. Its primary characteristic is isolation. There are no roads, fences or urban sprawl to give a point of reference. There is no one to hear your cries for help. You are alone. All alone! It is frightening, disorienting and painful. Yet it is here that many of us find ourselves and we cry for help, but there is no one to care. We cry out "Lord, Help! Why have you allowed this?" but all we hear is the pounding in our chest. Otherwise, silence. Have you been there? Are you there now?

God's purpose in bringing us into the wilderness is not to punish us. The penalty for our offenses was nailed to the cross at Calvary. Rather, He brings us here to isolate us from the damaging influences that estrange us from Him. There He speaks comfort to us and sustains us through all our trouble. As believers, we are the Bride of Christ and He is the "Lover of our souls". His purpose is to establish an intimate relationship with us and thereby restore true joy.

It's all about Him! And so I focus my attention on Him and His Word. He becomes the central theme of my preoccupation. In doing so, my personal disappointments are overshadowed by His presence. He outshines my hurts as does the noonday sun outshine the faint flickering of a distant candle.

For I reckon that the sufferings of this present time are not worthy to be compared with the glory which shall be revealed in us. (Romans 8:18)

WOW! These are WordsOfWisdom we can live by >>)))*>

Personal Challenge And Prayer Of Commitment

No greater challenge for obedience and the solace that comes from submission can be found than that of the words of George Matheson (1882)

O Love That Will Not Let Me Go.

O Love that will not let me go,
I rest my weary soul in Thee;
  I give thee back the life I owe,
That in thine ocean depths its flow
    May richer, fuller be.

O Light that followest all my way,
I yield my flickering torch to Thee;
  My heart restores its borrowed ray,
That in Thy sunshine's blaze its day
    May brighter, fairer be.

O Joy that seekest me through pain,
I cannot close my heart to Thee;
  I trace the rainbow through the rain,
And feel the promise is not vain
    That morn shall tearless be.

O Cross that liftest up my head,
I dare not ask to fly from Thee;
  I lay in dust life's glory dead,
And from the ground there blossoms red
    Life that shall endless be.

I tell you the truth, unless a kernel of wheat falls to the ground and dies, it remains only a single seed. But if it dies, it produces many seeds. The man who loves his life will lose it, while the man who hates his life in this world will keep it for eternal life (John 12:24-25)

"Dear Lord, forgive me for my self-centeredness. Work out Your will in me to make me a vessel of honor. In Jesus Name, Amen."

Chapter 26

I THINK IT'S ALL OVER, AND THEN &
THE REVITALIZATION OF FAITH

LOVE STORY – I Think It's All Over, And Then ...

The sun was setting in the cool Colorado evening behind the backdrop of blue mountains whitened with snow, and silhouetted against pastel crimson sky. I stood alone by her grave and had my final conversation with my Darling.

"I know you're not here Sweetheart. But I need to say some things, for my sake. There is such a big hole in my life since the Lord took you. I think that I am over it, and then ... and then I am overcome with uncontrollable grief. I watch archeologists dig ancient ruins of an old city on the Discovery Channel, and I cry. I see a road construction crew building a new bridge, and I cry. A tumbleweed blows across the highway in front of my car and I cry. There is no logical reason for my despondency, except that the light of my life has flickered out. Maybe if I hadn't loved you so dearly, the hole would not be as gigantic. My mind replays the countless blessed memories of times we enjoyed together and I miss you so much. Nothing can fill the vacancy you left. But then, of course you know that.

"I am so grateful to God that you are not here to bear this

grief. I would never want to see you hurt like this, so I praise God that He took you first. The kids and I are doing well. You would be real proud of me. I am doing a lot of writing, just like you said I would. Soon I shall be on the road again. I am praying that the Lord will open new doors of ministry for me. The valley that the Lord has taken me through has deepened my relationship with Him. It will be a new Wilf that enters the lecture's stand. My desire is to be only where the Lord places me and speak only those things that He directs me.

"Thank you my Darling for this conversation. I guess it is more of a soliloquy, a dramatic monologue. Maybe my talking to myself is a catharsis, just a means that brings about release from my concerns. In any case, I feel much better now.

"Oh, one last thing. My remains shall join yours soon, and I see that I will be laid to rest on your right-hand side, the way it has been for the last forty-four years. Good night my Darling. See you in the morning!"

I make a quality choice to turn my face away from the morbid preoccupation of "Camelot" past, and look to the "Glories" of the future. God is not through with me yet. Both joy and responsibility await me and I eagerly turn my face toward that. With Christ, life is beautiful!

God's character has never changed. I find Him to remain faithful. Because He is *the God that healeth thee* (Exodus 15:26) I shall never cease to pray and believe for miracles like healing. The outcome is His responsibility. It is He that chooses the path that each must follow. An old hymn summarizes God's leading well.... *some through the waters, some through the flood, some through great sorrows but all through the blood!* The operative word in this hymn is through. He will take you through. Through whatever! Thanks to the prayers of the saints and His constant presence, I am coming <u>through</u> remarkably well and becoming a better person for having had the experience.

My sincere prayer is to relate the comfort and encouragement that I have received to others that may find themselves in similar circumstances. This is the reason for WOW (WordsOfWisdom).

Now WOW - The Revitalization Of Faith

Another full moon! Each month I see a full moon and I am reminded of... of.... But then, how can anyone forget significant events when they are associated with specific stimuli. People that were alive when President J.F. Kennedy was assassinated can remember the time and place where they were when they heard the news.

The flight of the Space Shuttle Challenger began at 11:38 a.m. on January 28, 1986 and ended 73 seconds later with an explosion of hydrogen and oxygen propellants. The T.V. images are forever etched on our memories. In memory of the seven astronauts that perished that day, President Ronald Reagan wrote a fitting tribute. "The future is not free: the story of all human progress is one of a struggle against all odds. We learned again that this America, which Abraham Lincoln called the last, best hope of man on Earth, was built on heroism and noble sacrifice. It was built by men and women like our seven star voyagers, who answered a call beyond duty, who gave more than was expected or required and who gave it little thought of worldly reward." - President Ronald Reagan (January 31, 1986)

Everyone can recall where they were when they heard the news that the space shuttle Columbia and the crew incinerated during reentry above Texas, just 16 minutes before landing on February 1, 2003. And I, every time I witness the rise of a full moon I am reminded of that hospital room and my beloved Donna.

"Am I locked forever into this painful memory," I ask

myself? "Will every full moon turn me into some mythical monster that wallows among the dark shadows of yesteryear?" "It is time that the full moon remind me of better things," I think. Then it suddenly dawns on me that this is a month of the Blue Moon.

The expression, "once in a blue moon" comes from the fact that a blue moon appears a total of seventeen times every 20 years. A blue moon is the second full moon in the same calendar month. For a blue moon to occur, the first of the full moons must appear at or near the beginning of the month so that the second will fall within the same month. Because a full moon appears every 29.5 days, a blue moon is extraordinary.

Yes, another moon! This is not some sign or omen or divine epiphany. It is simply a reminder that new beginnings and opportunities present themselves on a daily basis, and they that are locked into the past will find ample reminders to imprison them there. It for this reason that the writer of Hebrews challenges us, *Wherefore seeing we also are compassed about with so great a cloud of witnesses, let us lay aside every weight, and the sin which doth so easily beset us, and let us run with patience the race that is set before us,* <u>*Looking unto Jesus*</u> *the author and finisher of our faith; who for the joy that was set before him endured the cross, despising the shame, and is set down at the right hand of the throne of God.* <u>*For consider him*</u> *that endured such contradiction of sinners against himself, lest ye be wearied and faint in your minds.* (Hebrews 12:1-3)

The sun gives needed light by day for life. Full moons are placed in the darkened skies to give us light by night. The Son of Righteousness enlightens every dark shadow of life and revitalizes our purpose for being. What a wonderful God we serve! *...in Him we live and move and have our being...* (Acts 17:28)

Of course, we are living in the flesh, but we do not fight in a fleshly way. For the weapons of our warfare are not those of the flesh. Instead, they have the power of God to demolish fortresses. We tear down arguments and every proud obstacle that is raised against the knowledge of God, taking every thought captive in order to obey Christ. (2 Corinthians 10:3-5)

WOW These are **W**ords**O**f**W**isdom we can live by! ><)))*>

A Personal Challenge And Prayer Of Commitment

Finally, my brethren, be strong in the Lord, and in the power of his might. (Ephesians 6:10) Now unto him that is able to keep you from falling, and to present you faultless before the presence of his glory with exceeding joy, To the only wise God our Saviour, be glory and majesty, dominion and power, both now and for ever. Amen. (Jude 1:24-25)

"Dear Lord, I rejoice in You. You are the light of life. In You I shall live and move and have my being. I shall not forget all Your benefits towards me. My life shall be a reflection of Your presence. Bless the Lord Oh my soul! – Amen."

Chapter 27

A Legacy For Our Children
Michelle, Adrienne, Stephen, Jennifer

Michelle

I'm sitting in my bedroom and I can hear my teenage children laughing with their friends. They hold their attention with stories of when they were little. "Remember when...?" Then laughter erupts and a warm smile breaks across my face.

I too, remember when. I remember when my Mom would call me every day and say, "Good Morning, Honey. What's on your agenda for today?" We would frequently get together in the afternoon and run off to a store or plant flowers or whatever.

Someone told me these memories will make me laugh some day. Right now, they make me lonely and I don't much want to laugh. With the passing of time, I don't cry as much. There is sun on the horizon.

One of the last moments I spent with Mom, I snuggled up to her neck. I said, "Mom, you know how momma's love the smell of their babies? Well, babies love the smell of their mammas too", and I inhaled the scent of my Mom. I didn't want to stop. I was afraid that if I stopped she would die and so would I.

The loneliness was overwhelming, after Mom passed. I wanted to talk to her. My entire being ached to be with her and I wanted to smell her fragrance. Then it dawned on me how much the Lord wants us to desire the same of Him. He longs for us to yearn for Him.

My Mom and Dad had a wonderful relationship with each other, but more than that, they had a yearning to know and serve their Heavenly Father. They gave us a wonderful heritage and many memories that keep us laughing.

Mom and Dad never compromised. Regardless of their difficulties, Mom never complained and her tears were few. Their faith carried them through their hardships.

Dad continues the journey without Mom. His faith and trust in the Lord sustains him. We cry together. We pray together. We worship together and yes, we also laugh together. I am blessed because I was given the life I have.

Thank you Mom for your example and the laughter and tears we shared together. Mine is a rich heritage.

Adrienne

Dear Mom

My final tribute is the last letter I will ever write you. I've been thinking of you all day today. It's six months to the day since the Lord took you home. I miss you so much. Mom, I want to thank you for all that you gave me and all that you were to me. As a young girl, I envisioned you as T.V. sitcom's June Cleaver, a perfect mom. But in my thirties you became to me what you had been all your life to a lot of other people; the most wonderful and dedicated friend.

You were such a good example of what true women of God should be. You taught me never to compromise and to stand firm in my faith. You also taught me that true happiness comes when we dedicate our lives to serving the Lord. You were such a great wife to dad and the kind of friend who was able to change people's lives just because they knew you. You were the best mom and grandmother that anyone could ever have asked for. I feel so fortunate that my children were able to have such a wonderful grandmother to look up to and admire.

Mom, I want to thank you for teaching me how to be a godly woman that loves her family and friends. I pray that when God calls me home, I will have impacted half as many lives as you have. I pray my children and grandchildren will see you through me, and that I too will leave them with the same kind of memories and heritage that you and Dad left me. I pray that my husband and I will have a Love Story that will be as beautiful and romantic as yours and Dads. Your love and legacy will live on in all the people you have touched.

Mom, I miss you so much that sometimes it hurts and there is not a day that goes by that I don't think about you. But praise God, He is alive, and because of His Son that shed His blood, I too someday will be standing by your side in His presence. So with this said, Mom I love you, and thank you Lord, how could I have I asked for more?

Thank you Mom. I love you! - Adrienne

Stephen

How surreal! The reality of chapters in life opening and closing seems so contrary to reason. It is hard to accept the finality of death. They say you can earn and lose fortunes many times in a lifetime, but you can never get back lost days, lost time.

My memories are so vivid and yet somehow like viewing a chapter that has been closed. I do remember being a tough young teenage boy who, when no one was looking, would curl up and let Mommy tickle him. The many trips you made to the hospital on my behalf must have driven you crazy. Mom, you stood up for me in the face of authorities because you believed what I was saying was true. You unconditionally loved me through those years when turning your back on my behavior would probably have been more appropriate. You then became my friend when that stage in life had passed. Above all, you were a living symbol of Christ by showing me Jesus in your selfless love.

The interaction between you and Dad and the relationship you had is a model for all married couples. How blessed we were to have had you. I guess it doesn't surprise me that God wanted your company. To me, you always were an angel on earth. You were loved and respected by all whose lives you touched. You will always be my mommy and I miss those chapters in my life where you were so involved. I am glad that when I get to heaven I'm going to be more than just a spirit, 'cause I'm going to need a big hug."

I will see you soon Mom.

Jennifer

I have always been concerned about the legacy that I would leave behind. What would people say and what would they remember me for. Will my children be a reflection of my beliefs and deepest dreams? Then, I think of my mother and realize that a legacy is not a conscious effort to perform but a quality of who we are.

My mother's legacy is my rich inheritance. From the shape of my triceps to my compassion and determination, I emulate her character. She was a woman of uncompromising devotion to God. If she questioned Him, we never saw it. Though her life was not perfect or without heartache, still she "lived" a life of faith and trust in God.

Her desire to serve the Lord and center her life in Jesus is her greatest contribution to my life. She displayed patience, compassion and a zest for life. She had an appreciation for the world around her. She gave me a good sense of humor, a love of life and a solid rock to stand on – Jesus.

So I continue the circle of life by teaching my children what my parents taught me. I now know that my grandmother lives in me as my mother will live on through my girls. My girls will live for Jesus, as will my grandchildren and the generations that follow them. This is my mother's legacy.

Thank you mom for being a Godly example to me! I shall always be grateful to God for giving you to me as mom.

Now WOW - Insights Through Faith

The insights I have gained through this experience are shared in my seminars, messages and writings. When she was first hospitalized, I sat by her bedside to write three articles on the <u>Struggles Of Faith</u>. How does one reconcile faith with reality? As the weeks passed by, it grew into a manuscript of 27 articles that I published as WOW (an acronym for Words Of Wisdom) on my E-zines emailing list. These now form the chapters of this book. Our love story was added to each chapter following her death.

It is fitting that I show my gratitude for the significant contribution that my friends and loved ones have made to my life. You have borne my burden with me, and in doing so you have lightened my load. Thank you.

I have been lost in a deep dark forest since my wife Donna changed her address to Glory. Having all the theological and psychological facts neatly arranged does little to fill a void so large as the one she left behind. Trying to find meaning for life during my wandering seemed futile and pointless. But it is here that meaning is found. I have learned many valuable lessons about God's Faithfulness, His Sovereignty and His Glory. Three things stand out predominantly.

1) He is always present in the midst of crisis. Jesus told his disciples to pass over the Sea of Galilee to the other side. (Mark 4:35-41) A relentless storm struck without warning and threatened to capsize their craft. Fear and panic overwhelmed the disciples as they call, *"Master, carest thou not that we perish?"* Jesus awoke from his sleep, spoke calm to the wind and the waves and assured his followers with these words. *"Why are ye so fearful? How is it that ye have no faith?"*

There was no pressing need that required them to leave for the other side right then. It would have been rationally prudent for them to leave the next day. Furthermore, when they got there the disciples accomplished little of any value. Logically, the entire event appeared pointless. Then why the urgency to leave then? Why jeopardize the ship and the life in it?

The value of this experience was the journey. The lessons they learned proved to be invaluable. First, they learned that Jesus was present in every crisis. Secondly, they witnessed Jesus casting out the evil spirits from a demon possessed man. Thirdly, they discovered the power and authority that was at their disposal over circumstances and demonic opposition. Fourthly, they experienced the tremendous length and enormous cost involved in reaching one person. When they reached the other side, Jesus ministered to an audience of one! Finally, they learned that the effort they expended in delivering one man, resulted in many turning to Jesus. When he was healed and in his right mind, he went to Decapolis, a region of ten cities and preached ...*how great things Jesus had done for him.*

2) As God, He has the right to do what He deems best. He alone is God. One hundred sixty one times He declares,

I am the LORD *thy God! All things were made by Him and without him was not anything made that was made.* (John 1:3) *For by him were all things created, that are in heaven, and that are in earth, visible and invisible, whether they be thrones, or dominions, or principalities, or powers: all things were created by him, and for him: And he is before all things, and by him all things consist.* (Colossians 1:16-17) *For in him we live, and move, and have our being...*(Acts 17:28) *...O LORD, thou art our father; we are the clay, and thou our potter; and we all are the work of thy hand.* (Isaiah 64:8) *...this is the decree of the most High ... all the inhabitants of the earth are reputed as nothing: and he doeth according to his will in the army of heaven, and among the inhabitants of the earth: and none can stay his hand, or say unto him, What doest thou?* (Daniel 4:24, 35) *What then shall we say? Is God unjust? Not at all! "I will have mercy on whom I have mercy, and I will have compassion on whom I have compassion." It does not, therefore, depend on man's desire or effort, but on God's mercy ... But who are you, O man, to talk back to God? "Shall what is formed say to him who formed it, 'Why did you make me like this?' Does not the potter have the right to make out of the same lump of clay some pottery for noble purposes and some for common use?* (Romans 9:14-21)

No further commentary can add to the undeniable fact that God is Sovereign. We therefore willingly yield to His sovereign will, knowing that His mind is preoccupied with our best welfare. *What is man, that thou art mindful of him ...* (Psalms 8:4) *For I know the thoughts that I think toward you, saith the LORD, thoughts of peace, and not of evil, to give you an expected end. Then shall ye call upon me, and ye shall go and pray unto me, and I will hearken unto you. And ye shall seek me, and find me, when ye shall search for me with all your heart. And I will be found of you, saith the LORD: and I will turn away your captivity...* (Jeremiah 29:11-14)

3) All things are created for His glory. Jesus and His disciples encounter a man who was blind from birth. *"Master, who did sin, this man, or his parents, that he was born blind,"* they asked him? (John 9:1-3) Jesus answered, *Neither hath this man sinned, nor his parents: but that the works of God should be made manifest in him.* The man was healed, but his blindness was for God's glory.

Lazarus was sick and his sisters Mary and Martha summons Jesus. (John 11:1-4) He waited two days to make His "house call" during which time Lazarus died. Why the delay? Why allow the pain, the worry and the trauma to continue? The answer is clear. *This sickness is not unto death, he said, but for the glory of God, that the Son of God might be glorified thereby.* Lazarus was sick, died and raised to life, all to the glory of God. I like the end of the story, but if he had not been raised to life, his sickness would still have been to the glory of God.

Peter was offended when Jesus asked him, *Do you love me?* Jesus this did three times. Then Jesus told him that as a young man he dressed himself and went where he well pleased, but that the day would come when another would clothe him and lead him where he didn't want to go. *This spake he, signifying by what death he should glorify God.* (John 21:15-19) Death is a means to glorify God? Indeed, with life and with death, we shall bring glory to Him. Peter spent his entire life with the vivid memory of God's call ... *feed my sheep!* Everything is about Jesus.

I shall always have faith in God's ability to heal sickness and disease. I am firmly committed to the fact that God's desire for us is for good and not bad. His Word is filled with principles for life, health and well-being. A person that violates an established principle will suffer harmful effects. A good example is gravity. This law of the universe is irrevocable. Step from a second-story window and gravity will pull you downward to a painful landing. The laws of God's Kingdom have similar consequences. The Bible clearly states that obeying God's laws produce health, prosperity and well-being.

It must be remembered however, these are principles and not guarantees. You cannot reduce God to a formula that guarantees success. Solomon recognized this to be a fact when he lamented, *I returned, and saw under the sun, that the race is not to the swift, nor the battle to the strong, neither yet bread to the wise, nor yet riches to men of understanding, nor yet favour to men of skill; but time and chance happeneth to them all.* (Ecclesiastes 9:11)

Conclusion

Our knowledge, tightly constructed formulae and good works guarantee us one reward, and that is hell. Everything that we will ever own and become, is granted by God's grace alone. *For the wages of sin is death; but the gift of God is eternal life through Jesus Christ our Lord.* (Romans 6:23) Paul's testimony underscores this truth. *But by the grace of God I am what I am: and his grace which was bestowed upon me was not in vain; but I laboured more abundantly than they all: yet not I, but the grace of God which was with me.* (1 Corinthians 15:10) *Now this is our boast: Our conscience testifies that we have conducted ourselves in the world, and especially in our relations with you, in the holiness and sincerity that are from God. We have done so not according to worldly wisdom but according to God's grace.* (2 Corinthians 1:12)

Perhaps we place too great an emphasis our personal goals and comfort. Suffering for Christ's sake is not a popular topic in a society that champions independence as our ultimate achievement. Paul sought the Lord to remove his "inconvenience", but listen to his testimony. *And he* [Jesus] *said unto me, My grace is sufficient for thee: for my strength is made perfect in weakness. Most gladly therefore will I rather glory in my infirmities, that the power of Christ may rest upon me.* (2 Corinthians 12:9) In a similar way, we place entirely too much emphasis on life. The Book of Revelation speaks of the "over-comers" with these words, *And they overcame him by the blood of the Lamb, and by the word of their testimony; and they loved not their lives unto the death.* (Revelation 12:11)

Perhaps death is also given too great as significance well. Rather than seeing death in terms of cessation, it is time we championed the event as life's inauguration. *Behold, I show you a mystery; We shall not all sleep, but we shall all be changed, In a moment, in the twinkling of an eye, at the last trump: for the trumpet shall sound, and the dead shall be raised incorruptible, and we shall be changed. For this corruptible must put on incorruption, and this mortal must put on immortality. So when this corruptible shall have put on incorruption, and this mortal shall have put on immortality, then shall be brought to pass the saying that is written, Death is swallowed up in victory. O death, where is thy sting? O grave, where is thy victory? The sting of death is sin; and the strength of sin is the law. But thanks be to God, which giveth us the victory through our Lord Jesus Christ. Therefore, my beloved brethren, be ye stedfast, unmoveable, always abounding in the work of the Lord, forasmuch as ye know that your labour is not in vain in the Lord.* (1 Corinthians 15:51-58)

WOW   These are WordsOfWisdom we can live by.
><)))*>

End

Printed in the United States
24485LVS00001B/607-627